The World of Crypto and The Digital Wave

How to Invest in Cryptocurrency Wisely and Safely

before attempting any techniques outlined in this book.
By reading this book, the reader agrees that under no circumstances is the author responsible for any direct or
indirect losses incurred as a result of the use of the information within this book, including, but not limited to, errors, omissions, or inaccuracies.

This book is dedicated to everyone who has made lots, lost lots, and could have made lots of money because of timing. Many investors who began this journey without awareness lost their bitcoins and crypto wallets. This book is dedicated to you and future investors of cryptocurrencies.

Table of Contents

Introduction

I vividly recall a late November night, the air chilly, and my eyes fixed on the computer screen. The numbers danced, and my heart raced as I executed my first successful cryptocurrency trade. It wasn't just about the profit. I realized I was part of a more significant movement—a financial revolution reshaping our understanding of money. At that moment, I ignited a journey into the fast-paced, often unpredictable world of digital currencies. This personal journey, brimming with excitement and learning, is what I'm thrilled to share with you.

Over the past three years, I've navigated the crypto markets on platforms like Robinhood, Coinbase, Crypto.com, and Uphold. These experiences have taught me not only how to trade successfully but also how to do so securely. I've learned the importance of keeping private keys safe. Private keys are essentially the passwords that give you access to your cryptocurrency holdings, and losing them could mean losing your investment. I've also learned the critical need to understand the risks tied to online exchanges. There were many lessons; some were learned the hard way, but each was invaluable.

This book was born from a passion for sharing these insights with you. Its purpose is simple yet vital: to guide you in investing in cryptocurrency wisely and safely. Knowledge of protecting your investments is crucial in a landscape of potential and peril. The potential is the opportunity for significant financial gain, but the peril is the risk of losing your investment due to market volatility, security breaches, or regulatory changes. We will explore strategies to ensure your digital assets remain secure, and I'll share the practices that have worked for me.

Cryptocurrency can be daunting. The technical jargon, the fear of financial loss, and the volatile nature of the market can be intimidating. Many hesitate to enter this space, fearing that they will need more knowledge to succeed. This book aims to dispel those myths and make crypto accessible to everyone. We will break down the barriers preventing many from benefiting from this transformative technology.

What sets this book apart is its foundation in real-world experience. I won't just share theories or abstract concepts. You'll find practical, actionable advice drawn from my journey. We'll explore real-world case studies, dissect up-to-date market trends, and navigate the maze of exchanges and security protocols. This guide is firmly rooted in reality and designed to give you the necessary tools to succeed. With this practical advice, you'll feel more than ready to embark on your cryptocurrency journey, confident that it's been tested in the real world.

As you read, I invite you to see yourself in these pages. Whether you are a curious newcomer or a cautious skeptic, this book speaks to you. We'll explore scenarios and questions that resonate with adults from all walks of life, helping you find your place in the crypto landscape.

The book is structured to gradually and comfortably take you from a beginner to an informed investor. We'll start by understanding the crypto landscape, then move to setting up accounts and navigating markets. We'll delve into ensuring security so your investments remain protected. Each section builds on the last, guiding you step by step. This approach ensures you'll never feel overwhelmed and always be in control of your learning, providing a comfortable and reassuring learning experience.

Please take the first step in your cryptocurrency journey and prepare your mind to enter the world of digital currencies confidently. The future of finance is digital, and now is the time to be part of this exciting evolution. Welcome to a journey of discovery, opportunity, and empowerment.

Chapter 1: Understanding the Cryptocurrency Landscape

As I recall that pivotal moment, I find myself in awe of how the seemingly abstract world of cryptocurrencies has become an integral part of our financial systems. It's hard to believe that what started with a single Bitcoin transaction has grown into a global phenomenon. The evolution of digital currencies is fascinating and a testament to the power of innovation. This chapter aims to unravel the complexities and wonders of the cryptocurrency landscape, a realm that continues to captivate and challenge investors worldwide.

1.1 Decoding Blockchain: The Backbone of Cryptocurrency

At the heart of every cryptocurrency lies a marvel of modern technology: the blockchain. This decentralized ledger records transactions across a computer network, ensuring it remains unalterable once data enters the chain. Imagine a series of blocks containing a batch of transaction data linked together in a chain. These blocks are cryptographically secured, making tampering with the information they contain nearly impossible. This immutability is a cornerstone of blockchain's integrity, offering a level of security that traditional databases cannot match.

Blockchain technology is a game-changer in data storage and management. Instead of traditional databases that rely on a central authority, blockchain's decentralized nature is its unique selling point. This means no single entity controls the ledger, spreading control across a network of participants. This enhances security and transparency and revolutionizes how we think about data management. Proof of Stake and Proof of Work ensures that all investors agree to the validity of transactions, maintaining the integrity of the blockchain. Excluding the need for intermediaries, blockchain reduces costs and risk,

offering a more efficient and secure alternative for transaction processing.

The blockchain world is diverse, with various types catering to different needs. Blockchains like Bitcoin and Ethereum are open to almost everyone, allowing participants to join and contribute to the network. These platforms provide transparency and security, making them ideal for open financial systems. In contrast, private blockchains restrict access and are typically employed by enterprises seeking secure, internal data management solutions. Consortium blockchains offer a middle ground where organizations govern the network, balancing transparency with controlled access. Each type serves specific use cases, illustrating the versatility of blockchain technology to cater to a wide range of needs.

Despite its growing prominence, blockchain often faces misconceptions. Many still assume it's synonymous with cryptocurrencies, overlooking its broader applications in healthcare and supply chains. Blockchains securely store data, not just financial transactions. Some confuse blockchain with distributed ledger technology (DLT), though blockchain is a type of DLT distinguished by its unique structure and cryptographic features. Understanding these nuances helps demystify blockchain, revealing its potential beyond cryptocurrencies.

Blockchain's transformative potential extends far beyond digital currencies. Its decentralized nature makes it a robust platform for innovation, offering a secure and transparent method for conducting transactions. Whether used to track supply chains, secure healthcare records, or facilitate cross-border payments, blockchain provides reliable data management that challenges traditional systems. It offers unbanked populations financial services, highlighting its capacity to drive positive change. As we explore the intricacies of blockchain, we uncover a technology with the power to redefine industries and empower individuals, demonstrating its broader applications and potential to drive positive change.

This potential should inspire us all, promising a more dynamic and inclusive financial future.

By understanding the intricacies of blockchain technology, you gain insight into the foundation of cryptocurrencies and their broader implications. This knowledge equips you to navigate the crypto landscape confidently, appreciating blockchain's security and efficiency. As you delve deeper into digital currencies, you'll find that the blockchain is more than just a technological marvel; it's a gate to an innovative era of financial alternatives. Its security and efficiency reassure you of its potential, making you feel confident in its role in the future of finance.

1.2 Cryptocurrency Types: Beyond Bitcoin

Bitcoin stands as the inaugural beacon of the cryptocurrency revolution, a creation by the enigmatic figure Satoshi Nakamoto that brought the concept of digital currency into mainstream consciousness. Its introduction marked a pivotal shift from traditional financial systems, offering an alternative form of value exchange rooted in cryptography and decentralization. Often heralded as "digital gold," Bitcoin has become a store of value, much like precious metals, due to its limited supply of coins. This scarcity and the robust security of its network have allowed Bitcoin to maintain a dominant position in the market, drawing attention and investment from around the globe.

However, the landscape of digital currencies extends far beyond Bitcoin, offering a myriad of altcoins, each bringing unique features and innovations. Ethereum, for instance, has carved out a niche with its groundbreaking intelligent contract functionality. Unlike the Bitcoin platform, Ethereum enables developers to build decentralized applications (dApps) on its platform, effectively creating a programmable blockchain. This flexibility has spurred a wave of innovation, particularly in decentralized finance (DeFi), where traditional financial services are reimagined without intermediaries. Then there's Ripple, which focuses on revolutionizing cross-border payments. By facilitating nearly instantaneous transactions with minimal fees, Ripple aims to replace the cumbersome and costly processes associated with traditional banking systems. Meanwhile, Litecoin offers faster transaction speeds, making it a practical choice for everyday transactions and a favored option for those seeking efficiency in their exchanges. The diversity of these options is not just intriguing; it's exciting, offering a wide array of opportunities for everyone interested in the cryptocurrency market.

In the diverse ecosystem of cryptocurrencies, stablecoins hold a particularly crucial role. These digital currencies are pegged to stable assets like the US dollar to mitigate the volatility of cryptocurrencies. Tether, one of the most prominent stablecoins, exemplifies this concept by maintaining a consistent value relative to the dollar. Stablecoins are invaluable in the crypto market, serving as a haven during volatile periods and a reliable medium for trading and remittances. They bridge the gap between the unpredictable world of cryptocurrencies and the stability of traditional fiat currencies, providing a sense of security for investors and traders alike.

The cryptocurrency venue keeps growing, with new trends and innovative cryptocurrencies hinting at the future of digital finance. Crypto coins like Monero and Zcash have gained attention for their ability to provide anonymous transactions, a feature increasingly valued in our privacy-conscious era; they use advanced cryptographic techniques to ensure that transaction details remain hidden, appealing to users who prioritize confidentiality. Furthermore, the field of tokenomics and DeFi is rapidly advancing, introducing novel concepts like yield farming and liquidity mining. These innovations allow users to earn rewards by providing liquidity to decentralized exchanges or participating in network governance, demonstrating the potential for cryptocurrencies to serve as a medium of exchange and generate passive income. This forward-thinking approach to digital finance is not only optimistic but also promising the way for a more dynamic and inclusive financial future.

As we explore these diverse facets of digital currencies, it becomes clear that the world of cryptocurrency is not static but dynamic and ever-changing. Each coin and token brings something different, contributing to a vibrant and multifaceted ecosystem that challenges the status quo of typical general finances. This diversity offers endless possibilities for both innovation and investment, paving the way for new forms of financial interaction that are more inclusive, efficient, and secure. In this rapidly growing alternative financial exchange, staying informed is crucial to navigating and capitalizing on cryptocurrency opportunities.

1.3 The Mechanics of Mining: How New Coins Are Created

The concept of cryptocurrency mining is as fascinating as it is intricate. At its core, mining involves intriguing growth and building to validate and record transactions on the blockchain. This process is crucial, as it ensures the integrity and security of the network. Miners, essentially the backbone of this digital ledger, perform these computations using powerful computers. It is solved, then a new block is added to the blockchain, where the miner receives new coins. This incentivizes miners to continue supporting the network, making mining both a critical function and a financial opportunity.

Mining employs consensus mechanisms to maintain the blockchain's reliability. The most common is Proof of Work (PoW), which Bitcoin uses. Miners are required to compete to solve cryptographic puzzles, which demand significant computational power and energy. In contrast, Proof of Stake (PoS) offers an alternative by selecting validators based on coins they stake as collateral. PoS is less energy-intensive and allows faster transaction processing, appealing to newer cryptocurrencies focused on sustainability and scalability. Each method has benefits and drawbacks, influencing how miners approach their tasks.

To participate in mining, one must invest in specific hardware and software. Application-Specific Integrated Circuits (ASICs) are highly efficient machines designed for PoW mining, particularly for Bitcoin. They offer superior performance but come with a hefty price tag. On the other hand, Graphics Processing Units (GPUs) provide flexibility, allowing miners to switch between different cryptocurrencies. While less powerful than ASICs, GPUs are more accessible and can be used for other computing tasks. Alongside hardware, mining software is crucial, enabling miners to connect to the blockchain network, join mining pools, and optimize their operations.

Mining's environmental impact has sparked significant debate. Bitcoin mining, for instance, consumes high amounts of energy, which leads to concerns about carbon emissions and sustainability. The industry's response has been varied, with some initiatives focusing on renewable energy sources to power mining operations. Efforts to transition to less energy-intensive consensus mechanisms, like PoS, also aim to mitigate environmental damage. These green solutions highlight the ongoing tension between technological advancement and ecological responsibility, a balance the industry continues to navigate.

Economically, mining presents both opportunities and risks. Miners earn block rewards and transaction fees, which can be lucrative, especially when cryptocurrency prices are high. However, the volatility of these prices poses a significant challenge. Mining profitability can fluctuate dramatically, influenced by market trends and the cost of electricity. As a result, miners must constantly evaluate their strategies, balancing operation costs with potential returns. For many, it is a high-stakes endeavor requiring careful planning and adaptability.

Mining's complexity and challenges mirror the broader dynamics of the cryptocurrency world. It demands technical knowledge, financial understanding, and a willingness to adapt to changing conditions. Yet, for those who succeed, mining offers financial rewards and a sense of contributing to a groundbreaking technological movement. As we continue to explore the intricacies of cryptocurrency, the role of mining remains central, a testament to the innovative spirit that drives this digital frontier.

1.4 Nodes and Networks: The Pillars of Decentralization

Imagine a bustling city where each building represents a node in a blockchain network. Just as each building plays a role in the city's ecosystem, each node contributes to the blockchain's functionality and security. These nodes, acting as individual computers connected to the network, perform tasks ranging from validating transactions to a copy of the entire blockchain storage. Full nodes are like skyscrapers, housing comprehensive data and ensuring the network's robustness. They check each transaction against the blockchain's rules, maintaining the ledger's integrity. Light nodes, on the other hand, function like smaller offices. They rely on full nodes for data validation but offer convenience and speed for everyday tasks. The diversity of these nodes—each with its strengths—enhances the network's resilience, much like a city thrives on its varied infrastructure.

As transactions occur within this digital city, nodes collaborate to validate them, ensuring the network's integrity. This process resembles a neighborhood watch, where community members collectively verify activities. Nodes use consensus mechanisms to agree on which transactions are legitimate. This consensus process involves complex algorithms that confirm the accuracy of transactions before adding them to the blockchain. Once validated, these transactions become part of an immutable ledger, much like a city archive that records every event. This collective agreement system eliminates the need for a central authority, fostering a sense of trust and security among participants.

Decentralization stands as a beacon of security and trust in blockchain systems. In traditional networks, a single point of failure can lead to catastrophic consequences, akin to a blackout in a city reliant on one power plant. Blockchain's decentralized nature disperses control, preventing any entity from manipulating data. This creates a trustless system where transactions occur without intermediaries, akin to neighbors trading directly without an intermediary. The absence of central control enhances security, as there's no single target for malicious attacks. Trust emerges organically from the network's structure, reassuring participants that their transactions are safe and reliable.

However, decentralized networks face challenges that test their scalability and efficiency. As more participants join, the network can experience congestion, similar to rush hour traffic in a growing city. This congestion poses the scalability trilemma— a balancing act between security, decentralization, and scalability. Finding equilibrium among these factors is crucial to maintaining a network that can grow without compromising security or decentralization. Solutions like sharding divide the network into smaller, manageable segments, allowing for parallel processing of transactions. Layer 2 protocols, akin to an express lane in traffic, aim to alleviate congestion by collectively processing transactions off the main blockchain and placing them on record. These solutions offer hope for addressing scalability issues, ensuring decentralized networks can accommodate growth while retaining their fundamental principles.

As blockchain technology evolves, nodes remain central to its operation, embodying the decentralized ethos that underpins the system. By understanding the role of nodes, we gain insight into the mechanics of blockchain networks and their potential to reshape industries. The interplay between nodes, transactions, and decentralization forms the backbone of this transformative technology. As we embrace the possibilities of blockchain, we step into a world where trust, security, and innovation converge, paving the way for a future that challenges conventions and empowers individuals. We glimpse the intricate dance of technology and community through the lens of nodes and networks. This dance promises to redefine how we interact and transact in the digital age.

Chapter 2: Setting Up for Success

Imagine facing a massive digital market, bustling with opportunities yet fraught with risks. The growth potential is immense, but so are the pitfalls for the unwary. This chapter guides you in navigating this complex terrain, starting with choosing a secure cryptocurrency exchange. This choice can differ between a rewarding experience and a disastrous loss. Exchanges act as your gateway to digital currencies, facilitating the buying, selling, and trading various tokens. However, not all exchanges are created equal. Selecting a reputable one is crucial for secure and successful trading.

The history of cryptocurrency is littered with tales of exchanges that fell prey to security breaches. These incidents have left investors wary and serve as stark reminders of the risks involved. One infamous example is the Mt. Gox hack, which lost millions of dollars worth of Bitcoin. This breach shattered exchange trust and highlighted the importance of robust security measures. When choosing an exchange, reputation is paramount. It's essential to scrutinize user reviews and ratings, as these can provide insights into the platform's reliability and user experience. A platform's reputation often reflects its commitment to security and customer service, making it a critical factor in your decision-making process.

Trustworthy exchanges possess several key characteristics that set them apart. A user-friendly interface is one such feature, ensuring beginners can easily navigate the platform. An ingenious design lessens the learning curve and empowers you to focus on trading rather than grappling with complex systems. Additionally, liquidity and trading volume are vital indicators of an exchange's credibility. High liquidity means you can execute trades swiftly without causing significant price fluctuations, while substantial trading volume reflects the platform's popularity and trust within the community. These components facilitate seamless trading experiences and enhance your ability to capitalize on market opportunities.

Regulatory compliance is another essential aspect of a secure exchange. Adherence to legal standards indicates that the platform operates within a framework designed to protect investors. Familiarize yourself with the exchange's Know Your Customer (KYC) and Anti-Money Laundering (AML) policies. These policies are in place to prevent fraud and secure rightful users only. Additionally, inquire about the exchange's insurance policies for user funds. While cryptocurrency exchanges are not Securities Investor Protection Corp. members, some platforms offer insurance to cover potential losses due to theft or hacking. This added layer of security can provide peace of mind as you engage in trading activities.

Consider the following checklist as a practical tool to assist you in evaluating potential exchanges. Transparency of fees is crucial; hidden fees can erode your profits and lead to frustration. Ensure the exchange outlines its fee structure, including deposit, withdrawal, and trading fees. Customer support and dispute resolution are equally important. Expedient and effective customer service can make a massive difference in the event of a fraudulent act. Seek other formats of support to access assistance when needed. These elements combined will guide you in selecting an exchange that aligns with your needs and trading goals.

Checklist for Evaluating Exchanges

- **Reputation:** Check user reviews and the platform's rating.

- **User Interface:** Ensure it's intuitive and easy to navigate.

- **Liquidity & Volume:** Look for high liquidity and substantial trading volume.

- **Regulatory Compliance:** Verify KYC and AML policies.

- **Insurance Policies:** Ask about insurance for user funds.

- **Fee Transparency:** Confirm the clarity of fees.

- **Customer Support:** Find available and supportive channels.

These policies and support systems will help you make proper decisions and set the stage for a successful cryptocurrency trading experience.

2.2 Wallets 101: Hot vs. Cold Storage Solutions

Cryptocurrency wallets are the bedrock of any digital asset strategy, pivotal in storing and managing your investments. Unlike exchanges, which facilitate the buying and selling of cryptocurrencies, wallets are solely dedicated to holding your digital coins. This distinction is crucial because while exchanges can be convenient for trading, they are not inherently secure for long-term storage. A personal wallet ensures that only you can access your assets, minimizing the risk of loss due to an exchange breach or shutdown. It's akin to keeping your money safe at home rather than leaving it at a bank where you can only indirectly oversee its security. Understanding these differences is fundamental to protecting your investments.

Regarding cryptocurrency wallets, the choice often boils down to hot versus cold storage solutions. Hot wallets connected to the internet are designed for easy access and quick transactions. They resemble mobile apps or web interfaces, like Coinbase Wallet or MetaMask, providing a seamless way to manage your day-to-day transactions. However, this connectivity comes with a trade-off. Being online makes hot wallets more vulnerable to hacking attempts, akin to leaving your purse on a café table.

On the other hand, offline cold wallets are the go-to long-term storage option. These can be hardware devices resembling USB sticks, Zor or Ledger, or even paper wallets. Cold storage is immune to online threats, making it highly secure for safeguarding your assets over extended periods. It's like placing your valuables in a locked safe, away from prying eyes.

Security considerations for each wallet type are paramount. While hot wallets offer convenience, their vulnerability to cyber threats cannot be underestimated. Hackers constantly seek ways to exploit online systems, and if your hot wallet is compromised, your assets could be at risk. Cold wallets, by contrast, excel in security due to their offline nature. They are less susceptible to hacking but require careful handling and storage. Losing a cold wallet or its recovery phase means losing access to your funds permanently. Thus, it's essential to back up your cold wallet and place it in a very secure location, much like you would safeguard crucial documents.

To ensure the safety and accessibility of your digital assets, adhere to best practices for wallet management. Regularly updating your wallet software and firmware is critical to defending against vulnerabilities. Developers usually release updates to patch security flaws, and staying current can protect your assets from emerging threats. Additionally, employing solid and unique passwords is a must. Complex passwords give extra account security. Enabling security features like two-factor authentication (2FA), where available, also enhances protection. This simple step can thwart unauthorized access, even if your password is compromised. Lastly, diversify your storage approach. Use hot wallets for routine transactions and reserve cold wallets for long-term holdings, balancing convenience and security. By following these guidelines, you can navigate the world of cryptocurrency with greater confidence and peace of mind.

2.3 Creating Your First Cryptocurrency Account: A Step-by-Step Guide

Setting up your first cryptocurrency account is a significant step that opens the door to digital assets. The process begins with selecting a cryptocurrency exchange that aligns with your goals. Once you've chosen an exchange, the next step is registering your essential information, like your name, email address, and a secure password. Choosing a strong password and combining letters, numbers, and symbols are necessary to enhance security. After submitting this information, you'll likely receive a confirmation email. Then, you will follow the instructions from your email to activate your account. This step is crucial as it ensures the exchange recognizes your identity, laying a foundation for secure transactions.

The registration process is only the beginning. Next, you'll need to complete the identity verification process, often called KYC or Know Your Customer. This step requires you to provide the required documentation, usually a government-issued ID. While this might seem tedious, it's necessary to safeguard your account and comply with regulatory standards. Verifying your identity enhances security and unlocks additional features on the exchange. For instance, verified accounts typically enjoy higher withdrawal limits, allowing you to access your funds more freely. Moreover, should any issues arise, having a verified account facilitates account recovery. This layer of security ensures that your assets remain protected, granting you peace of mind as you navigate the crypto landscape.

With your account verified, it's time to set up payment methods, usually by linking your bank account or credit card to the exchange, enabling you to purchase cryptocurrencies. Bank transfers often have lower fees but can take longer to process, while credit cards offer instant transactions but may incur higher charges. You can choose the best preference that suits your needs. When linking a payment method, ensure that all transactions are secure. Look for exchanges with encryption and other security measures to protect your financial data. Verified payment methods streamline the buying process and add extra security to your transactions, reducing the risk of fraud.

Once your payment methods are in place, focus on securing your account. Start by revisiting your password and security questions. These should be unique and complex, discouraging unauthorized access. Use a password manager if necessary to keep track of your credentials. Immediately enable two-factor authentication (2FA). This requires a second verification form when you log in, giving you added security. 2FA protects and reduces unauthorized access to your accounts, even if your password is compromised. Most exchanges offer this feature, and activating it is a straightforward process that significantly enhances your account's security.

By taking these steps, you've laid a solid foundation for your cryptocurrency endeavors. The initial setup might seem meticulous, but a small investment of time pays off in security and peace of mind. As you progress in your cryptocurrency journey, remember that vigilance and proactive management of your accounts are essential. Always keep informed of security updates and adapt as the digital landscape evolves. When your account is securely set up, you will be ready to explore the opportunities that cryptocurrencies offer, equipped with the knowledge and tools to confidently navigate this exciting new frontier.

2.4 Two-Factor Authentication and Beyond Enhancing Account Security

In the digital world, safeguarding your cryptocurrency accounts is paramount. Two-factor authentication, or 2FA, is a simple yet powerful tool that protects against unauthorized access. When you enable 2FA, gaining access to your account requires more than a password. You also need a second verification form, which significantly reduces the risk of breaches. There are different types of 2FA methods, with SMS and authenticator apps being the most common. While
SMS-based 2FA sends a verification code to your phone, authenticator apps generate timesensitive codes that are more secure. Authenticator apps, such

as Google Authenticator or Authy, are less vulnerable to interception than SMS, making them a preferred choice for securing sensitive accounts.

Beyond 2FA, other advanced security measures can further fortify your account. Biometric authentication is one such method, using facial recognition or fingerprints to verify identity. This technology is becoming more prevalent, offering a seamless and secure way to access accounts. Security keys also provide robust protection. These hardware devices, such as YubiKeys, plug into your computer or phone and require physical presence to authorize transactions. They are particularly effective against phishing attacks, as they cannot be easily duplicated or intercepted. Integrating these technologies into your security routine can significantly enhance your account's defenses against threats.

Regular security audits are essential for maintaining account security. Just as you would routinely check your home's locks, reviewing your digital security settings is vital. Look for any unusual activity, such as unrecognized logins or transactions, and report them immediately. Keeping your personal information up-to-date ensures you can recover your account swiftly. This practice also helps maintain your account's integrity, as malicious actors can exploit outdated information. Regularly assessing your security settings allows you to adapt to new threats and update your defenses accordingly.

To help you implement these strategies, consider this checklist for maintaining account security. Regular password changes are essential for extra protection on your accounts. Stay vigilant against phishing scams, often disguised as legitimate communications from exchanges or service providers. Learn to recognize common signs, such as urgent requests for personal information or unfamiliar links, by remaining cautious and informed; this will protect you from potential scams. Together, these practices form a comprehensive approach to securing digital assets, ensuring you control cryptocurrency investments.

- **Enable 2FA:** Prefer authenticator apps over SMS for added security.

- **Use Biometric Authentication:** Implement if available on your devices.

- **Employ Security Keys:** Consider using hardware security keys for critical accounts.

- **Conduct Regular Security Audits:** Routinely review account activity and information.

- **Change Passwords Regularly:** Create strong, unique passwords using a password manager.

- **Be Aware of Phishing Scams:** Recognize and avoid suspicious emails and links.

With these measures in place, you can navigate the world of digital currencies with greater confidence and peace of mind. Embracing these security practices protects your investments and empowers you to explore cryptocurrency opportunities. As you continue to build your knowledge and skill, remember that staying one step ahead of potential threats is critical to success in this dynamic environment.

Chapter 3: Navigating the Market

Imagine being on a cruise ship, navigating through a sea of information, the horizon dotted with opportunities and challenges. In cryptocurrency, understanding market movements is akin to reading the stars for guidance. It demands a blend of skill, intuition, and the right tools. This chapter will navigate you through the meaning of reading cryptocurrency charts, a vital skill for anyone looking to make informed trading decisions. As a beginner, grasping the basics of technical analysis can seem daunting, but it's a journey worth taking. This approach uses historical data to anticipate future price movements, like a sailor predicting weather patterns based on past storms.

At the heart of technical analysis are candlestick patterns, which provide visual cues about market sentiment. Each candlestick represents price movement within a specific time frame, offering insights into whether the market is bullish (expected to rise) or bearish (expected to fall). For instance, a long green candlestick indicates intense buying pressure, suggesting a bullish market, while a long red candlestick points to selling pressure and a bearish trend. Understanding these signals is crucial for making strategic decisions, allowing you to enter or exit trades opportunistically. Alongside candlestick patterns, support and resistance levels are key concepts. Support is a price level where demand supports the price from dipping further down, while resistance is where selling pressure might stop the price from rising. Identifying these levels helps you pinpoint potential entry and exit points, enhancing your trading strategy.

Different types of charts offer various perspectives on market trends. Line charts, for instance, provide a simple view of overall price movements over time, ideal for spotting long-term trends. On the other hand, bar charts give more detail, showing opening and closing prices and highs and lows during intraday, days, weeks, and months. These charts are helpful for traders who need a deeper understanding of price fluctuations and their implications. Studying these chart types allows you to tailor your analysis to suit your trading style and objectives.

Technical indicators and oscillators are invaluable tools in your analytical arsenal, helping assess market conditions and potential price changes. Moving averages, for example, smooth out price data, allowing you to identify trends and possible reversals. A rising moving average suggests a bullish trend, while a falling one signals a bearish market. Another powerful tool is the (RSI) measuring the speed and change of price movements. It indicates whether a cryptocurrency is overbought or oversold, helping you gauge market momentum and make informed trading decisions. Integrating these indicators into your analysis provides a more comprehensive view of market dynamics, enabling you to navigate the crypto space confidently.

To illustrate the application of these tools, consider Bitcoin's historical price movements. During its 2017 bull run, Bitcoin's price increased to forecasted highs, driven by market hype and increased adoption. By analyzing candlestick patterns and moving averages, traders could identify critical support and resistance levels, making intelligent choices of when to buy or sell. Similarly, Ethereum's price surge in recent years offers another example. As smart contracts gained popularity, Ethereum's value increased, with technical indicators highlighting potential entry points for savvy investors. These real-world scenarios demonstrate how technical analysis can expand your knowledge of market trends and improve trading outcomes.

Exercise: Practice Analyzing a Crypto Chart

1. **Choose a Cryptocurrency**: Select a popular cryptocurrency like Bitcoin or Ethereum.

2. **Find a Reliable Chart**: Use a platform like TradingView or CoinMarketCap to access detailed charts.

3. **Identify Candlestick Patterns**: Look for bullish or bearish patterns within a specific time frame.

4. **Determine Support and Resistance Levels**: Mark these key price points on the chart.

5. **Apply Technical Indicators**: Use moving averages and RSI to assess market conditions.

6. **Make a Hypothetical Trade**: Based on your analysis, decide on potential entry and exit points.

Practicing these steps regularly will help you hone your analytical skills, empowering you to make proper decisions while you navigate the dynamic world of cryptocurrencies.

3.2 Bull Runs and Bear Markets: Identifying Market Cycles

In the landscape of cryptocurrency, market cycles are as inevitable as the changing seasons. Understanding these cycles is crucial for any investor seeking to navigate the complexity of digital assets. Market cycles typically consist of several phases, each with characteristics and implications for trading strategies. For example, the accumulation phase is when savvy investors quietly gather assets at lower prices, often unnoticed by the broader market. This phase can present an excellent buying opportunity, as prices have typically stabilized after a previous decline, setting the stage for potential growth. As the cycle progresses, the market enters the distribution phase, characterized by increased trading activity and optimism. During this time, prices may peak as investors begin to sell off assets, anticipating a downturn. Recognizing these phases allows you to make informed decisions, maximizing your potential gains while minimizing risks.

Bull and bear markets are distinct environments within these cycles, requiring different approaches. Rising prices and widespread investor optimism define a bull market. In this environment, confidence is high, and many traders are eager to buy in, hoping to capitalize on upward trends. However, it's important to remain cautious and avoid getting swept up in the euphoria, which can lead to overvaluing assets. Conversely, bear markets are marked by declining prices and general pessimism. During these periods, fear and uncertainty can lead to significant sell-offs as investors try to cut their losses. While bear markets can be challenging, they also offer opportunities for those who remain calm and strategic. By understanding the traits of each market, you can better position yourself to take advantage of the opportunities they present.

Navigating these market cycles requires a strategic approach. One effective method is dollar-cost averaging—investing money on set dates, not based on market conditions. This strategy allows you to purchase more assets when prices are low and fewer when prices are high, ultimately reducing the impact of volatility. Another helpful tool is the stop-loss order; it is sold automatically when it reaches a set price. This can help limit potential losses during downturns, providing a safety net when market conditions worsen. These strategies allow you to manage risk and protect your investments, even in unpredictable markets.

Looking back at historical examples can provide valuable insights into market cycles. The 2017 Bitcoin bull run remains one of the most significant events in cryptocurrency history. Driven by increased adoption and media attention, Bitcoin's price skyrocketed to nearly $20,000, creating a frenzy among investors eager to join the rally. However, this was followed by the 2018 crypto winter, a prolonged bear market that saw prices plummet and many investors face substantial losses. This cycle underscored the importance of understanding market dynamics and the need for strategic planning. By learning from these past events, you can better prepare for future cycles, ensuring that you make the most informed decisions possible.

3.3 Using Real-Time Data: Tools and Platforms for Staying Informed

In the fast-paced world of cryptocurrency, real-time data is your compass. It guides each decision, ensuring you act swiftly and accurately. Imagine you're a sailor navigating unpredictable seas; market news acts like the wind, influencing the direction and speed of your journey. Similarly, updating the latest cryptocurrency trading could be the difference between gains or losses. Prices fluctuate wildly with every news release, making timely access to information crucial. Liquidity data also plays a pivotal role in trading decisions. It tells you how easily an asset can be bought or sold. High liquidity means less price slippage and more stability, allowing you to execute trades confidently and efficiently.

To stay informed, turning to reliable platforms is essential. CoinMarketCap is a go-to source for market cap and price updates, offering a comprehensive overview of the crypto market's current state. It allows you to track the performance of various cryptocurrencies, compare them, and make informed decisions based on real-time data. For those focused on technical analysis, TradingView is an invaluable tool. Its advanced charting capabilities and a wide range of technical indicators empower traders to study market trends and identify various trading opportunities. Providing access to a wealth of data and insights, these platforms help you keep your mind on the market's movement, enabling you to act swiftly and strategically.

Advanced traders often use API data feeds to automate data retrieval and enhance their trading strategies. APIs, or Application Programming Interfaces, allow you to access real-time data directly from exchanges, providing constant information. This can be a game-changer, especially if you set up alerts for price changes. Imagine receiving a notification when a cryptocurrency reaches your target price, allowing you to act immediately. Furthermore, like humans, bots can execute trades based on pre-set criteria, reducing the necessity for constant manual monitoring. This automation can enhance efficiency and precision, enabling you to focus on strategy rather than the minutiae of every trade. Integrating these technologies into your trading routine allows you to streamline your processes and capitalize on market opportunities more effectively.

However, the abundance of information available can sometimes be overwhelming. With countless data points and news updates flooding in, it's easy to feel lost in the noise. Setting up custom dashboards can be incredibly helpful in managing this. These dashboards allow you to tailor your view, focusing only on the most relevant and essential information. You can filter out unnecessary clutter by prioritizing data sources based on reliability and relevance. Choose platforms and tools with a proven track record for accuracy and timeliness, ensuring that the data you rely on is trustworthy. This approach reduces distractions and enhances your ability to make informed decisions, keeping you grounded amid the whirlwind of market information.

Navigating the crypto market requires a balance of speed and discernment. With the right tools and strategies, you will stay ahead of the standards and make informed and timely trade executions that coincide with your mission.

3.4 FOMO Management: Making Decisions Without Pressure

Imagine standing on a crowded trading floor, the air buzzing with excitement and tension. In cryptocurrency, the sensation of FOMO, or the fear of missing out, is powerful. It's an emotional trigger that can lead to impulsive and often irrational decisions, akin to jumping on a bandwagon because everyone else seems to benefit. This psychological impact is to be considered. It can cloud judgment, pushing you to buy into a rapidly rising asset without thorough analysis, driven by the fear of missing out on potential gains. This cycle of hype and panic selling can create a volatile environment where decisions made in haste lead to regret.

Adopting strategies that promote discipline and rationality in investing is crucial to managing FOMO effectively. One effective technique is setting clear investment goals and adhering to them by defining what you aim to achieve, whether a specific return on investment or a particular portfolio composition. This clarity helps you resist the urge to chase every market trend. Practicing mindfulness and emotional regulation can also be invaluable. By remaining aware of your emotional state and how it influences your decisions, you can take a step back and evaluate whether your actions align with your long-term objectives. Stepping away from trading for a moment can help regain composure and perspective. Taking several long deep breaths, meditation, or just some quiet time for yourself is helpful.

Focusing on a long-term investment mindset is another antidote to FOMO. This approach emphasizes the benefits of patience and strategic planning over short-term gains. HODLing, or holding onto assets through market fluctuations, embodies this philosophy in the cryptocurrency community. It encourages investors to weather the storms of market volatility, confident in the potential for long-term growth. Diversifying portfolios is also a critical component. By spreading investments across various assets, you reduce the risk associated with any single one, providing a buffer against market swings. This strategy minimizes potential losses and allows you to exploit different growth opportunities.

Real-life scenarios highlight the significant financial outcomes that can result from FOMO-driven decisions. The 2017 ICO boom serves as a poignant example. During this period, the excitement of initial coin offerings led many to invest without due diligence. The allure of quick profits overshadowed the need for careful analysis, resulting in substantial losses for those caught in the frenzy. Similarly, recent surges in meme coins illustrate the volatility of markets driven by social media hype. While some investors experienced momentary gains, others faced steep declines when the bubble burst. These cases underscore the importance of maintaining a balanced perspective and a well-thought-out strategy.

Navigating the cryptocurrency market requires a measured approach. By understanding the psychological impact of FOMO and exercising strategies to mitigate its effects, you can make decisions that fit your financial goals and risk tolerance. The lessons learned from past market behavior are valuable guides, helping you stay grounded and focused amid the market's noise. As you continue to explore the potential of digital assets, remember that success often lies in the ability to think long-term, remain disciplined, and adapt to changing conditions. With these principles in mind, you are better equipped to make informed choices, fostering a resilient approach to investing in cryptocurrencies.

As we conclude this chapter, remember that understanding market dynamics and managing emotions are essential to successful trading. Equipped with these insights, you're ready to explore the next steps in your cryptocurrency adventure.

Chapter 4: Strategic Investment Approaches

Imagine yourself standing on a bustling trading floor, the air thick with anticipation and the hum of market activity around you. The cryptocurrency trading world is similar, with its rhythm and pace, demanding keen awareness and strategic thinking. Here, one of the most critical decisions you'll face is choosing between long-term and short-term investment strategies. Each path offers unique opportunities and challenges, shaping how you interact with the market and influencing your profit potential. As we explore these avenues, you'll discover how to craft a strategy that aligns with your personal goals and risk tolerance, guiding you toward successful outcomes in this dynamic financial landscape.

Long-term and short-term investments serve distinct purposes, each with its own set of objectives and potential outcomes. Long-term investing, often called HODLing in the crypto community, focuses on building wealth over time. This approach involves holding onto assets for several years, allowing them to appreciate as the market matures and the technology behind them develops. It's akin to planting and patiently tending to a seed, trusting it will grow into a robust tree over time. On the other hand, short-term investments capitalize on market volatility, seeking quick gains from price fluctuations over shorter periods. This strategy requires constant vigilance and adapting swiftly to changing conditions. It's like riding the waves of a turbulent sea, where skill and timing are crucial to success.

Both approaches come with their own set of benefits and risks. Long-term investments offer the advantage of reduced stress from market fluctuations. Concentrating on the more significant aspects of life gives you peace of mind during a volatile market and confidence in the potential for long-term growth. This strategy aligns well with a passive investment style, emphasizing fundamental analysis and understanding the project's potential and technology. However, longterm investments can be less liquid, making it harder to access funds quickly. They also require due diligence to avoid holding assets that may lose value over time. In contrast, short-term investments offer the allure of high returns through frequent trading, but they involve higher exposure to market volatility. This approach demands constant market monitoring and a keen understanding of technical analysis, with the added complexity of navigating potential tax implications.

Choosing the right strategy involves aligning it with your financial goals and risk tolerance. Begin by assessing your objectives. Are you aiming for rapid profits or focused on building a sustainable economic future? Consider your time commitment and resources. Short-term trading requires significant time and effort, while long-term investing demands patience and the ability to withstand market turbulence. Examining this perspective will help you decide which approach best suits your lifestyle and aspirations. Additionally, consider the tax implications of each strategy, as they can impact your overall returns. Thorough research and staying informed are essential for making sound investment decisions and ensuring your plan aligns with your goals and risk tolerance.

To illustrate these concepts, let's look at some real-world examples. Bitcoin's long-term growth trajectory serves as a compelling case study. Despite periods of significant volatility, those who held onto Bitcoin over the years have seen substantial returns, as the cryptocurrency has become an integral part of the financial ecosystem. This long-term vision requires patience and conviction, qualities that have rewarded steadfast investors. In contrast, altcoin day trading strategies highlight the potential for short-term gains. Traders who successfully capitalize on market movements leverage technical analysis to make informed decisions, often yielding impressive returns. These strategies require a complete understanding of market dynamics and a willingness to act swiftly, showcasing rewards and short-term trading pitfalls.

Reflection Section: Crafting Your Strategy

- **Define Your Financial Goals**: Are you focused on long-term growth or short-term gains? Write down your objectives and how they align with your lifestyle.

- **Assess Your Risk Tolerance**: Reflect on your comfort level with market volatility. Would you prefer a more stable approach, or are you open to taking risks for higher returns?

- **Consider Your Time Commitment**: How much time can you dedicate to monitoring the market and managing your investments?

Write down your reflections and revisit them as you continue to refine your investment strategy.

4.2 Diversifying Your Portfolio: Balancing Risk and Reward

Imagine yourself as a juggler skillfully balancing multiple balls in the air. This is akin to managing a diversified cryptocurrency portfolio. Diversifying is crucial in managing assets, a strategy that can stabilize your investments by reducing the impact of volatility associated with individual assets. No juggler relies on a single ball, so no investor should stake everything on one cryptocurrency. Investing in various digital assets will mitigate risks and enhance your portfolio's resilience. This approach cushions your portfolio against the wild swings that characterize the crypto market, helping you weather downturns more effectively.

In cryptocurrency, diversification means more than just holding multiple coins. It involves allocating funds across a broad spectrum of digital assets, like Bitcoin and Ethereum, alongside promising altcoins offering unique technologies or market potential. This strategy ensures that you're adequately exposed to the fortunes of a single coin. Including stablecoins in your portfolio is another effective method of diversification. These digital currencies are pegged to stable assets, such as the US dollar, reducing exposure to market swings. They act as a buffer, providing stability in turbulent times and a reliable means of preserving value when the market becomes unpredictable.

Beyond the confines of cryptocurrencies, exploring cross-asset diversification can further balance your portfolio. This approach involves incorporating traditional asset classes, such as stocks and bonds, which can offset the inherent volatility of digital currencies. By blending the predictability of conventional investments with the innovation of cryptocurrencies, you create a more balanced financial strategy. Real estate and commodities are also worth considering. These asset classes often move independently of crypto markets, providing additional security and potential growth avenues. This holistic view of investing acknowledges that while cryptocurrencies offer exciting opportunities, traditional assets remain crucial for long-term stability.

Constructing a diversified portfolio requires thoughtful planning and strategic execution. Start by determining a suitable allocation model that agrees with your investment ideas and risk tolerance. For instance, you might allocate 50% of your portfolio to large-cap cryptocurrencies, 30% to emerging altcoins, and 20% to stablecoins. This investment strategy provides stability for growth while maintaining a safety net. Periodically adjusting your portfolio is vital for maintaining diversification. As market conditions change, so do the values of your investments. Periodically review your holdings to ensure they still reflect your intended allocation. Adjust as necessary to keep your portfolio aligned with your objectives, selling assets that have grown disproportionately and reinvesting in those that have lagged.

Checklist: Building a Diversified Crypto Portfolio

- **Assess Your Risk Tolerance**: Determine how much risk you're comfortable taking.

- **Allocate Across Cryptocurrencies**: Mix large-cap coins with promising altcoins.

- **Include Stablecoins**: Use them as a hedge against volatility.

- **Explore Cross-Asset Diversification**: Consider traditional assets like stocks and bonds.

- **Regularly Rebalance**: Adjust your portfolio to maintain your intended allocation.

By thoughtfully diversifying your investments, you can confidently navigate the crypto market's ups and downs, ensuring that your financial goals remain within reach. This strategy protects your assets and positions you to capitalize on the diverse opportunities within the financial landscape.

Evaluating Altcoins: Spotting Promising Opportunities

In the vibrant and ever-evolving world of cryptocurrencies, altcoins present various opportunities, each with risks and rewards. As you dive into this diverse market, understanding the criteria for evaluating altcoins is crucial. One of the primary factors to assess is market capitalization and trading volume. These metrics glance at a coin's size, liquidity, and popularity. A high market cap indicates a well-established coin, often with a stable position in the market, while robust trading volume suggests active interest and ease of trading. Both indicators of a cryptocurrency's potential stability and growth must be considered alongside other factors to paint a complete picture.

Technology and unique value propositions are also critical when assessing altcoins. The technology underpinning an altcoin can significantly influence its long-term viability and adoption. Look for altcoins that offer innovative solutions or improvements over existing blockchain technologies. Unique value propositions differentiate an altcoin, offering real-world applications or addressing specific industry problems. This could range from enhanced security features to increased transaction speeds. Backed by solid technological foundations and compelling value propositions, Altcoins is more likely to gain traction in a competitive market.

Beyond surface-level metrics, delve into the project fundamentals to gauge an altcoin's potential. This involves examining the team's expertise to execute the project's vision. A team with a solid technology and finance background and a history of successful projects can instill confidence in the altcoin's prospects. Additionally, scrutinizing the project's roadmap and development milestones is essential. A clear and achievable roadmap indicates a well-thought-out plan for growth and development, while regular progress updates and milestone achievements demonstrate commitment and transparency.

Conducting both technical and fundamental analysis is vital when evaluating altcoin performance. Start by examining the project's whitepaper, a comprehensive document that outlines the altcoin's purpose, technology, and vision. A well-written whitepaper can offer valuable insights into the project's goals and feasibility. Community engagement is another critical aspect to consider because it can provide helpful feedback to developers. On the technical side, altcoin indicators can be utilized to assess market trends and price movements. They inform you of entry and exit points, enhancing your trading strategy.

Case studies of successful altcoin investments offer lessons and inspiration. Ethereum's rise to prominence exemplifies the power of innovation. Initially launched with the revolutionary concept of smart contracts, Ethereum has become a cornerstone of the blockchain industry, enabling the development of decentralized applications (dApps). Its growth underscores the importance of technological advancement and a robust developer ecosystem. Chainlink provides another compelling example. By pioneering decentralized oracles, Chainlink has addressed a crucial gap in blockchain technology—securely connecting intelligent contracts with real-world data. This innovation has propelled Chainlink to the forefront of the altcoin market, showcasing how addressing specific industry needs can lead to success.

As you explore the world of altcoins, remember to remain diligent and analytical. Thoroughly evaluating each opportunity can help you navigate the complexities of the market, identify promising investments, and manage risks effectively. This approach enhances your investment strategy and engages you in making proper decisions on this incredible platform of alternative cryptocurrencies.

4.4 ICOs and Token Sales: Participating Wisely

Initial Coin Offerings (ICOs) and token sales have emerged as pivotal fundraising methods in cryptocurrency's continuous development and growth. These mechanisms allow new cryptocurrency projects to obtain capital by issuing digital tokens to investors in exchange for highranking (currently #1 and #2) cryptocurrencies like Bitcoin or Ethereum. Unlike traditional fundraising, which often involves venture capital or initial public offerings (IPOs), ICOs democratize investment opportunities, opening the door to diverse investors. The token offerings vary, including utility tokens that provide access to a platform's services, security tokens representing ownership stakes, and stablecoins pegged to traditional assets to minimize volatility. Each type serves a distinct purpose within the ecosystem, offering unique benefits and challenges.

Participating in ICOs offers the allure of high potential returns, primarily when investing early. Investors who identify promising projects before they gain mainstream traction can reap significant rewards as token values appreciate. However, this profit potential is accompanied by substantial risks. The decentralized nature of ICOs makes them fertile ground for scams and fraudulent schemes, as seen in numerous high-profile cases. An alarming number of ICOs need to follow through on their commitments, which creates financial losses for restless investors. This volatility highlights the importance of rigorous due diligence and cautious optimism when considering participation in token sales.

A structured approach to evaluating ICOs is crucial to navigating these waters safely. Start by analyzing the whitepaper, a document that outlines the project's goals, technology, and value proposition. A thorough whitepaper provides insight into the project's potential and feasibility as a foundation for your investment decision. Next, verify the credentials of the team behind the ICO. A proven, qualified team with successful ventures can instill confidence in the project's execution. Assessing partnerships and collaborations is equally essential, as reputable affiliations can enhance a project's credibility and access to resources. By scrutinizing these elements, you can gauge the legitimacy and viability of an ICO, reducing the likelihood of falling victim to scams.

The cryptocurrency landscape is replete with cautionary tales and financial success for some, and this requires careful evaluation. Binance Coin's ICO exemplifies the potential for success. Launched by the Binance exchange, it quickly became one of the most successful ICOs, with its token significantly appreciating value as the platform gained prominence. This success was attributed to a well-executed strategy, a strong team, and a clear vision. Conversely, the story of BitConnect serves as a stark warning. Promising high returns with little transparency, BitConnect collapsed amid allegations of being a Ponzi scheme, resulting in substantial investor losses. These examples highlight the divergent paths ICOs can take, reinforcing the need for discernment and vigilance.

As you consider participating in ICOs and token sales, remember that thorough research and due diligence are your best allies. Attracting high returns can be tempting, but the risks are equally significant. Carefully evaluating each opportunity, you can confidently steer the complexities of the current cryptocurrency opportunities by deciding what fits your goals and risk tolerance. This approach not only enhances your chances of success but also empowers you to contribute thoughtfully to the growth and innovation of the digital currency ecosystem. With these insights, you're better prepared to explore the next chapter, which delves into security and privacy measures, ensuring your investments remain protected in this dynamic landscape.

Chapter 5: Security and Privacy

Imagine your cryptocurrency holdings as a vault of digital treasures. The vault is protected not by steel walls but by an intricate system of cryptographic keys—your first line of defense in securing digital assets. Understanding how these keys function is crucial in safeguarding your investments. Cryptographic keys consist of two parts: public and private keys. Public keys, much like a bank account number, allow others to send funds to your wallet, but they cannot retrieve any funds themselves. They are openly shared and used for encryption and verification. On the other hand, private keys are the secret codes that authorize transactions. They are akin to your ATM PIN, giving you access to your assets and enabling you to prove ownership and approve transactions on the blockchain.

The creation and storage of private keys are of paramount importance. A private key is often a 256bit number, essential for securing transactions and proving ownership of digital assets. Losing this key is equivalent to losing access to your funds permanently, as it cannot be recovered or reset like a forgotten password. Thus, secure storage is critical. You can store private keys in various ways, each with its level of security. Options include paper wallets, which involve printing and storing your keys physically or using QR codes for easy scanning.

Hardware wallets store keys offline and offer robust security by keeping them away from internet threats. Managed by third parties, custodial wallets can relieve some of the burdens of key management, but they require trust in the custodian's security measures. Non-custodial wallets, where you retain complete control, demand careful handling of your keys.

The consequences of losing or exposing private keys are severe. If a private key falls into the wrong hands, your assets can be easily stolen, with little chance of recovery. Hackers constantly seek to exploit vulnerabilities, making it vital to protect your keys from unauthorized access. Strategies for storing private keys safely include using cold wallets, which store keys offline, providing an added layer of security. Cold wallets are less accessible but offer more excellent protection against online threats. Though more convenient for those who prefer online access, hot wallets require additional precautions, such as strong passwords and two-factor authentication. When choosing your storage method, weighing the trade-offs between convenience and security is crucial.

Different forms of key management offer varying levels of control and security. Hardware wallets, like Ledger and Trezor, are popular choices for secure key storage solutions. These devices store private keys offline, protecting them from malware and hacking attempts. Their robust security features make them ideal for long-term storage of significant amounts of cryptocurrency. Another vital aspect of key management is using seed phrases, which serve as recovery keys when you set up your wallet. It allows you to recover your wallet if it's lost or damaged. Keeping your seed phrase secure is just as important as your private keys. Store it in multiple secure locations, ensuring only you can access it. Avoid storing it digitally, where hackers could compromise it.

When generating cryptographic keys, it's essential to ensure they are solid and secure. Utilize secure key generation tools that create complex keys that are resistant to hacking attempts. Avoid predictable patterns or easily guessed passwords, as these can be easily exploited. Randomness is critical to creating secure cryptographic keys, which enhances complexity. Regularly update your keys and passwords to stay ahead of potential threats. By taking these steps, you can protect your digital assets and secure your cryptocurrency investments.

Checklist: Securing Your Cryptographic Keys
- **Use Hardware Wallets**: Store private keys offline for maximum security.

- **Secure Your Seed Phrase**: Store it in multiple, safe locations.

- **Generate Strong Keys**: Use secure tools and avoid predictable patterns.

- **Consider Cold Storage**: Use for significant amounts of cryptocurrency.

- **Regularly Update Security Measures**: Stay updated on best practices and threats.

-

5.2 Protecting Against Scams: Recognizing Red Flags

In the digital world of cryptocurrency, scams lurk like shadows, waiting to exploit the unwary. Among the most prevalent are phishing schemes, where fraudsters craft cunning traps to capture your wallet credentials. These scams often arrive disguised as emails or messages from legitimate sources, urging you to click a link or provide sensitive information. Once you comply, your private keys and assets may be compromised. Then there's the allure of Ponzi and pyramid schemes, which promise unrealistic returns on investment. These scams rely on new investors to pay returns to earlier ones, creating a façade of profitability until the inevitable collapse. Recognizing these tactics is crucial in safeguarding your investments.

Detecting and avoiding scams requires vigilance and a keen eye for detail. Analyzing the credibility of investment opportunities is the first step. Be wary of offers that appear too good to be true or promise guaranteed returns. Such claims often signal fraudulent intentions. Verify the authenticity of communication channels by checking the sender's email address and scrutinizing website URLs for discrepancies. Legitimate companies will use official domains and avoid high-pressure sales tactics. Always cross-reference information with trusted sources, ensuring you engage with genuine entities. You can prevent many common scams by remaining skeptical and conducting thorough research.

Community vigilance plays a pivotal role in preventing scams. Engaging with others in community forums and discussions helps inform and protect you against fraud. These platforms offer a space for sharing similar situations with others. You can protect yourself and others better by staying informed about emerging scams and tactics. Exposing illegal activity to authorities, such as financial watchdogs or consumer protection agencies, helps dismantle fraudulent operations. Your vigilance contributes to a safer environment, fostering a community of informed and cautious investors.

Real-life case studies offer poignant lessons on the impact of scams. The infamous Mt. Gox exchange hack is a sheer reminder of the vulnerabilities within the cryptocurrency ecosystem. When the largest Bitcoin exchange, Mt. Gox, was compromised in 2014, it lost approximately 850,000 Bitcoins. The hack shook the industry, highlighting the importance of robust security measures and due diligence. In another example, the OneCoin scam captivated investors with promises of a revolutionary cryptocurrency. However, it was later revealed as a Ponzi scheme, defrauding billions of unsuspecting victims. These cases underscore the need for caution and critical thinking when navigating crypto.

Case Study Reflection: The OneCoin Scam

- **Overview**: OneCoin marketed itself as a leading cryptocurrency, promising investors with high returns and revolutionary technology. However, it was revealed to be a Ponzi scheme, lacking a blockchain or genuine functionality.

- **Impact**: Estimated losses reached over $4 billion, affecting thousands of investors worldwide.

- **Lessons Learned**: Always verify a blockchain's existence; assess the project's transparency and its leaders' credentials. Avoid investments that lack clear, verifiable information.

These stories remind us that while the cryptocurrency landscape offers immense opportunities, it also presents risks that require careful navigation. By arming yourself with knowledge and staying connected to reputable sources, you can protect your digital assets from those who seek to exploit the uninformed.

5.3 Secure Wallet Management: Best Practices for Safety

Safeguarding your digital assets is paramount; therefore, wallet management is the cornerstone of security. Regular software updates are not just a recommendation; they are a necessity. Developers continually work to patch vulnerabilities and improve security features, making it imperative that you keep your wallet software current. Consider it routine maintenance for your car—neglecting it will cause unnecessary maintenance issues when you least expect it. Alongside these updates, consider employing multi-signature wallets. These require multiple approvals for extra security before any transaction can be processed. It's like requiring more than one key to open a vault, ensuring that no single point of failure can compromise your assets.

A vigorous backup and recovery strategy is vital for preventing losing access to your digital funds.

Creating secure backups of your wallet data is a foundational practice. Store these backups in multiple locations, both physical and digital, to protect against unforeseen events like hardware failure or data corruption. Implementing seed phrase recovery is another critical component; it acts as a master key, allowing you to recover your wallet if you lose entry to your primary device. Keep this phrase offline, written down, and stored securely in several safe places. Imagine it as a treasure map, invaluable but dangerous if it falls into the wrong hands.

Hardware wallets provide a vigorous security solution for those serious about long-term storage. Devices like Ledger and Trezor offer an effective means to keep your assets safe. They store your keys offline, away from the vulnerabilities of the internet. Setting up a hardware wallet requires initializing the device to generate a seed phrase and transferring your assets. The process is straightforward, but it demands careful attention. Once set up, you use the wallet to confirm physical transactions, adding another security layer. It's like having a safe for your digital gold, only accessible through your direct authorization.

Managing who has access to your wallet information is another critical aspect of secure wallet management. Limit access to only those you trust implicitly, as each additional person increases the risk of unauthorized actions. Monitor transaction approvals closely, ensuring that every outgoing transfer is intentional and verified. This oversight acts as a final safeguard against potential breaches. It is a security checkpoint where only approved transactions can pass. By maintaining tight control over access rights, you can better protect your digital assets from unauthorized use or theft.

Exercise: Assess Your Wallet Security

- **Update Software**: Check that your wallet software is the latest version.

- **Backup Data**: Ensure backups are stored securely in multiple locations.

- **Review Access Rights**: List who has access and assess if changes are needed.

- **Test Recovery**: Confirm you can recover your wallet using the seed phrase.

These foundational practices secure your assets and instill confidence in managing and protecting your digital wealth. With these measures in place, you are well-prepared to navigate the complexities of the cryptocurrency world, ensuring that your investments remain safe and accessible.

5.4 Privacy Coins: Ensuring Anonymous Transactions

In digital currencies, privacy coins stand out for their commitment to anonymity. Unlike regular cryptocurrencies like Bitcoin, which are pseudonymous and allow tracing through public ledgers, privacy coins conceal transaction details, offering a layer of confidentiality. The difference is vital for individuals and businesses seeking to protect sensitive financial information from prying eyes. Privacy coins are designed to obscure sender and receiver identities and transaction amounts, making them ideal for scenarios where discretion is paramount. For instance, they are beneficial in protecting personal privacy, conducting confidential business transactions, or operating in environments where financial freedom is restricted.

Due to their advanced technologies, Monero and Zcash have carved notable niches among the leading privacy coins. Monero utilizes cryptography to secure transaction anonymity. Ring signatures mix a user's transaction with others, creating a shroud of plausible deniability, while stealth addresses generate one-time addresses for each transaction, further masking the recipient's identity. These features make Monero highly effective at maintaining privacy. Zcash, on the other hand, uses zk-SNARKs, a form of zero-knowledge proof, allowing transactions to be verified without revealing the underlying data. This technology enables Zcash to offer shielded transactions, giving users a choice of privacy or transparency.

Using privacy coins comes with ethical and legal considerations. While they offer legitimate benefits, such as safeguarding personal data and ensuring transaction confidentiality, they also face regulatory scrutiny. Governments worldwide express concerns over their potential misuse of illicit activities, such as money laundering or tax evasion. Consequently, privacy coins are subject to varying legal statuses across different jurisdictions. Some countries may impose restrictions or outright bans, while others permit their use with specific regulations. Users must understand the legal landscape and their responsibilities when using privacy coins. Ethically, these coins should be used for legitimate purposes that respect privacy rights and comply with applicable laws.

To use privacy coins effectively, focus on maintaining security and compliance. Start by familiarizing yourself with the platforms and tools that support privacy coin trading. Ensure your transactions are conducted through reputable exchanges that adhere to legal standards. Consider splitting more significant amounts into smaller transactions to minimize traceability. Always verify the security features of your wallets, ensuring they support the anonymity aspects of the privacy coins. Furthermore, stay informed about the regulatory environment and emerging technologies that could impact the use of privacy coins. By balancing privacy with compliance, you can leverage the benefits of privacy coins while minimizing risks.

Privacy coins offer a unique approach to digital transactions, marrying advanced cryptographic techniques focusing on confidentiality. Their role in the cryptocurrency ecosystem underscores the ongoing tension between privacy and regulation. This chapter has explored how privacy coins work, their ethical and legal challenges, and their best practices. As we move forward, we will delve into the broader implications of cryptocurrencies, examining how they intersect with legal frameworks and what this means for investors and users. Understanding these dynamics will prepare you for the complexities of navigating this evolving financial landscape.

Chapter 6: Tax Implications and Legal Considerations

Picture this: the thrill of your first cryptocurrency gain, the numbers rising as you watch your investment grow. Yet, amid the excitement, a nagging question arises—how does this newfound wealth fit within the framework of tax regulations? Trying to maneuver your digital assets with taxes may feel uneasy, but understanding these rules is essential for any responsible investor. As cryptocurrencies become part of our financial culture, knowing how to report and manage these assets within the bounds of the law cannot be overstated.

Cryptocurrencies are considered financial instruments for tax purposes, not currency, as the IRS outlines. This classification signifies that gains or losses are subject to capital gains tax laws. You must report when you gain or lose by selling and buying cryptocurrency. If you sell a cryptocurrency and gain more than the purchase price, the difference is considered a capital gain; selling for less constitutes a loss. The IRS expects you to report these transactions on your tax return, just as you would with stocks or real estate. This distinction between property and currency is crucial, as it sets the stage for calculating and reporting gains and losses.

The tax implications of different cryptocurrency transactions can vary significantly. For instance, buying and selling cryptocurrencies is straightforward, but each transaction has tax ramifications. When you purchase crypto, you establish a cost basis, the asset's original value, for tax purposes. When you sell it, gain or loss is the difference in sale price and cost basis. Beyond simple trades, activities like mining and staking also have tax implications. Mining income is typically considered ordinary income, taxed at your regular income tax rate, while staking rewards can also be taxable, depending on the jurisdiction and specific circumstances. Both activities require careful recordkeeping to ensure accurate reporting.

Critical tax rules and exemptions play a pivotal role in how you manage your cryptocurrency investments. Capital gains tax may vary depending on how long an asset is held. Assets held for less than a year are taxed at ordinary income tax rates, considered short-term. Long-term gains, for assets held longer, benefit from reduced tax rates. This distinction encourages investors to consider longer holding periods to minimize tax burdens. Additionally, you may need to adhere to reporting requirements for foreign-held assets if you have cryptocurrency in foreign accounts. While the specifics can be complex, understanding these rules helps you align your investment strategies with tax obligations.

Timely and accurate tax reporting is critical to avoid penalties. The IRS sets specific deadlines for filing your annual tax return, typically by April 15th each year. Failing to report crypto transactions or underreporting can lead to fines and interest charges, compounding potential tax liabilities. To ensure compliance, keep detailed records of all transactions, including dates, amounts, and fair market values. This meticulous documentation simplifies tax filing and protects you during an audit. By staying organized and informed, you can confidently navigate the tax landscape, ensuring that your cryptocurrency gains contribute positively to your financial journey.

Reflection Section: Evaluating Your Crypto Tax Readiness

- **Record-Keeping**: Do you have a system to track all your crypto transactions? Consider using spreadsheets or crypto tax software to organize your data.

- **Understanding Tax Implications**: Are you aware of how each type of transaction affects your taxes? Consult your tax professional and inspect the IRS guidelines.

- **Filing Timeliness**: Have you marked the tax filing deadline on your calendar? Ensure you have ample time to gather your records and submit your return before the deadline.

6.2 Reporting Cryptocurrency Earnings: A Step-by-Step Guide

Imagine you've just completed a successful year of cryptocurrency trading. Your portfolio has grown, and it's time to face the task of reporting your earnings. This process begins with identifying taxable events, which are specific actions that trigger tax obligations. Any time you sell, exchange or even give away cryptocurrency, you create a taxable event. Such transactions need careful attention, as they determine the gains or losses you must report. Calculating these gains and losses involves knowing your cost basis—the initial value of your asset when you acquired it. Whether it was purchased, mined, or received as payment, this cost basis is essential for determining your financial outcome. When you sell, the difference between the sale price and the cost basis reflects your gain or loss, directly impacting your tax liability.

Accurate reporting hinges on thorough documentation. Maintaining detailed records of every transaction is not just a best practice—it's a necessity. Transaction logs and exchange statements are your primary tools for tracking your activities. They provide a chronological account of your trades, purchases, and sales. Receipts for crypto purchases and sales further support your documentation efforts, offering proof of the cost and nature of each transaction. This meticulous record-keeping not only aids in calculating your taxes but also protects you in the event of an audit. Think of it as building a financial map that charts the course of your cryptocurrency activities, ensuring that each step is accounted for and verifiable.

Navigating the complexities of crypto tax reporting can be daunting, but you can do it with others. A range of tax software options is available to simplify the process. Platforms like TurboTax Premium and Koinly provide user-friendly interfaces for tracking and reporting your crypto earnings. They automate much of the work, integrating with your exchange accounts to pull transaction data and calculate gains and losses. Hiring a crypto-savvy tax professional can be invaluable for those with more complex portfolios or a desire for personalized assistance. These experts offer tailored advice and ensure compliance with ever-evolving tax laws. Applying these aspects, you may improve your reporting process and focus more on managing your investments.

Despite the available resources, challenges in crypto tax reporting remain prevalent. One of the most common issues is handling transactions across multiple exchanges. Each platform may use different formats and standards, complicating the task of consolidating data. To manage this, consider using software aggregating transactions from various sources, providing a unified view of your activities. Airdrops and forks present another challenge. These events can result in receiving new tokens, which may be taxable as income at the time of receipt. Determining their fair market value requires careful assessment, often involving exchange rates or market data from the time of distribution. By addressing these challenges head-on, you can demystify the reporting process and ensure your tax obligations are met with minimal stress.

6.3 Navigating Regulatory Landscapes: Compliance Essentials

Navigating the global regulatory environment of cryptocurrencies is akin to charting a course through a sea of varying legal frameworks. Across the globe, countries approach cryptocurrency regulation in diverse ways, reflecting different priorities and levels of technological adoption. The SEC and CFTC play significant roles in shaping the regulatory landscape in the United States. The SEC protects investors and maintains fair markets, often scrutinizing Initial Coin Offerings (ICOs) under securities laws. Meanwhile, the CFTC oversees commodity and futures markets, which include certain cryptocurrency derivatives. This dual oversight creates a complex environment where understanding the nuances of each regulatory body is crucial for compliance.

Across Europe, the regulatory landscape varies widely. The European Union has made strides toward creating a cohesive regulatory framework through initiatives like the Markets in CryptoAssets Regulation (MiCA), which aims to standardize rules across member states. However, individual countries still need to retain the ability to impose regulations. In Asia, we see another spectrum of regulatory approaches. Countries like Japan have embraced cryptocurrencies with comprehensive regulatory measures, while others, like China, have taken a more restrictive stance, limiting or outright banning certain crypto activities. Learning to differentiate is vital for investors, as regulatory conditions can significantly impact the viability and legality of crypto investments in each region.

Staying informed about regulatory changes is not just a good practice; it's necessary for anyone involved in cryptocurrency. Regulations evolve rapidly, influenced by technological advancements, market dynamics, and political considerations. Monitoring updates from regulatory agencies ensures that you remain compliant and can anticipate how new laws might affect your investments. Subscribing to updates from official channels, such as the SEC or relevant European bodies, can keep you abreast of the latest developments. Additionally, understanding the impact of new laws on existing investments helps you adjust strategies proactively, mitigating risks associated with non-compliance or unexpected legal challenges.

Maintaining compliance in this shifting landscape requires a strategic approach. Adhering to Know Your Customer (KYC) and Anti-Money Laundering (AML) requirements is fundamental. Actions like these prevent illegal activities by ensuring that participants in the crypto market are correctly identified and vetted. Most exchanges now mandate KYC processes before allowing trades, making it a standard part of participating in the crypto ecosystem. Familiarizing yourself with these processes and ensuring that all necessary documentation is up to date is crucial. Additionally, reporting obligations for cross-border transactions must be observed, as many countries require detailed disclosures for international crypto activities. This includes understanding potential tax implications and ensuring that all transactions are accurately reported.

The benefits of regulatory compliance extend beyond avoiding penalties. Compliance enhances the legitimacy and security of your investments, fostering trust and confidence among other market participants. Investors who adhere to regulations are often seen as more dependable and create extra opportunities and collaborations. Furthermore, compliance grants access to regulated exchanges and financial services, which are generally more secure and stable than their unregulated counterparts. These platforms often offer enhanced security measures and insurance protections, providing additional safety for your assets. By embracing compliance, you safeguard your investments and ensure better growth and ability reliability in the cryptocurrency market.

6.4 Legal Pitfalls to Avoid: Staying on the Right Side of the Law

Cryptocurrency is ripe with promise yet carries its share of legal minefields. Among the most pressing concerns for investors is being scammed. These scams often offer enticing offers and seem too good to be true. They try to entice investors by promising high returns, leveraging the complexity and novelty of digital currencies to disguise their true intentions. Protecting yourself starts with a healthy dose of skepticism. Be cautious of schemes that guarantee profits or pressure you into making quick decisions. Thoroughly research any investment opportunity and remain wary of unsolicited offers, primarily through social media or email.

Another significant legal pitfall involves violations of securities laws, particularly with unregistered Initial Coin Offerings (ICOs). Many investors need to pay more attention to the regulatory requirements associated with ICOs, which can lead to unintentional violations. The SEC has clearly stated that many ICOs may qualify as securities, requiring proper registration and compliance with securities laws. Not adhering to regulations can result in punishable consequences for the issuers and investors. To avoid these pitfalls, ensure that any ICO you participate in is registered and compliant with applicable laws. This protects you from legal repercussions and financial loss should the ICO face regulatory sanctions.

Conducting due diligence is a foundational step in safeguarding your investments. Begin by evaluating the credibility of the project team and their advisors. Investigate their backgrounds, previous projects, and the reputation they hold within the industry. A solid group with a proven track record indicates a project's potential success. Next, review all legal documentation and disclosures associated with the investment. These documents should be transparent and clearly understand the project's objectives, risks, and regulatory compliance. Consider it a red flag if any documentation needs to be clarified or completed. Conducting thorough research minimizes risks and enhances your decision-making process, arming you with the necessary knowledge to invest wisely.

The consequences of non-compliance with crypto laws can be severe and far-reaching. Adherence to regulations can result in fines and penalties, quickly eroding any gains you might have achieved. Regulatory authorities may take legal action in more severe cases, leading to court proceedings and potential criminal charges. These outcomes can tarnish your reputation and create financial setbacks. Understanding the legal landscape and ensuring compliance is not just about avoiding these consequences; it's also about fostering trust and credibility within the industry. Adhering to regulations contributes to a more stable and secure market environment.

Finding legal advice and representation is a prudent step whenever you're uncertain about the legal implications of an investment. Choose a lawyer with expertise in digital currencies, as the nuances of cryptocurrency law differ from traditional finance. An expert attorney can provide guidance on compliance, help navigate complex legal frameworks, and represent you in disputes or regulatory inquiries. It's advisable to seek legal counsel when the stakes are high, such as when dealing with significant investments, participating in ICOs, or encountering potential legal issues. Having expert advice can be invaluable, offering peace of mind and ensuring that your interests are protected.

With the constant growth of cryptocurrency, being informed and cautious is vital. Understanding the legal pitfalls and taking proactive action will secure your investments and contribute to a healthier, more transparent market. Legal compliance safeguards your assets and positions you as a responsible participant in the crypto space.

Chapter 7: Real-Life Success Stories and Case Studies

In the early days of Bitcoin, when the concept of digital currency was beginning to ripple through the tech-savvy corners of the internet, a few daring individuals foresaw its potential and took a leap of faith. Among these pioneers was Laszlo Hanyecz, who etched his name into cryptocurrency history with a rather unassuming transaction. On May 22, 2010, Hanyecz made the first known purchase of a physical product using Bitcoin, exchanging 10,000 BTC for two pizzas. At the time, this amount equated to roughly $41, with each pizza costing about $25 when purchased by a British man on his behalf. While the price of Bitcoin has since skyrocketed, making those pizzas worth millions today, this transaction is celebrated annually as Bitcoin Pizza Day. Hanyecz expressed no regret over the purchase, viewing it as an experiment in a nascent financial system that few understood. His story reflects the early adopter's mindset: curiosity and willingness to engage with groundbreaking technology despite its uncertain future.

Similarly, the Winklevoss twins—Cameron and Tyler—recognized Bitcoin's potential early on, investing millions into the cryptocurrency when it was still in its infancy. Because Mark Zuckerburg had legal battles concerning Facebook, they turned their attention to Bitcoin, amassing a substantial holding that would later contribute to their recognition as Bitcoin billionaires. Their investment approach was methodical, driven by an understanding of Bitcoin's potential as a store of value and a hedge against inflation. They became vocal advocates for digital currency, founding the Gemini exchange to provide a secure platform for trading cryptocurrencies. Their venture undermines the relevance of strategic investment and foresight, qualities that have served them well in the volatile world of digital assets.

The early days of Bitcoin were fraught with challenges, not least of which was navigating regulatory uncertainty. Bitcoin operated outside traditional financial systems as a decentralized currency, prompting questions about legality and oversight. Early investors like Hanyecz and the Winklevoss twins often faced skepticism and misunderstanding. The absence of clear regulations posed significant risks as governments grappled with categorizing and regulating this new asset class. Additionally, the psychological impact of market volatility was immense. Bitcoin's price fluctuations were dramatic, with values soaring and plummeting seemingly overnight. Investors needed resilience to withstand these swings, maintaining confidence in Bitcoin's long-term potential despite short-term turbulence. The emotional rollercoaster of these early years tested their resolve, yet those who persisted often reaped substantial rewards.

From these early adopters, valuable lessons emerge for today's investors. Patience and a longterm vision are paramount. The journey of Bitcoin's pioneers illustrates the relevance of staying affirmative against adversity, recognizing that transformative technologies often require time to mature. This encourages investors to focus on the broader potential of digital assets rather than getting caught up in daily market fluctuations. Diversification also emerges as a critical strategy for mitigating risk. By spreading investments across various cryptocurrencies and other asset classes, investors can buffer against market volatility, ensuring that no single downturn devastates their portfolio. These principles are as relevant now as they were in Bitcoin's infancy, guiding investors toward thoughtful, informed decision-making.

Bitcoin's prominence is marked by several key milestones that underscore its growth and influence. One pivotal moment came when Bitcoin reached parity with the U.S. dollar, a symbolic achievement that signaled its acceptance as a viable currency. Media attention played a significant role in Bitcoin's adoption, as coverage of these milestones piqued public interest and drove further investment. News outlets and social media platforms amplified

Bitcoin's story, transforming it from a niche interest to a global phenomenon. This exposure accelerated its integration into mainstream financial discussions, paving the way for broader acceptance and use. These historical events highlight the interplay between innovation and public perception, illustrating how media can shape the trajectory of emerging technologies and their adoption.

7.2 Altcoin Successes: Stories Beyond Bitcoin

In the rapidly evolving world of cryptocurrencies, altcoins have carved out their niches, showcasing remarkable success stories that extend far beyond Bitcoin's shadow. Ethereum is a prime example, transforming the blockchain landscape with its pioneering intelligent contract technology. Unlike Bitcoin, which primarily functions as digital currency, Ethereum introduced a programmable blockchain that facilitates decentralized applications, or dApps. This innovation has opened countless possibilities, enabling developers to create applications independently of centralized authorities. Ethereum's rise can be attributed to its adaptability and the vibrant ecosystem it supports, making it a cornerstone of the crypto world. Its ability to automate transactions and agreements without intermediaries has captured the financial and tech sectors' imagination, catalyzing the rapid growth of decentralized finance (DeFi) and other blockchainbased services.

Ripple offers another compelling narrative, revolutionizing the way cross-border payments are conducted. By leveraging blockchain technology, Ripple has created a system that allows for nearinstant settlement of international transactions, a stark contrast to the traditional banking systems that often take days to process such payments. Ripple's success is built on its ability to address the inefficiencies plaguing global financial networks, offering a solution that is not only faster but also more cost-effective. This has positioned Ripple as a leader in the fintech space, with its impact resonating across financial institutions worldwide. By providing a seamless mechanism for currency conversion and fund transfers, Ripple has redefined the potential of cryptocurrencies in real-world applications, demonstrating the practical benefits of blockchain technology beyond speculative trading.

The unique value propositions of these altcoins lie in their ability to solve specific market needs. Ethereum's smart contracts automate complex processes, reducing the need for intermediaries and lowering transaction costs. This appeals to industries seeking efficiency and transparency. Ripple's focus on cross-border payments addresses a critical pain point for businesses and individuals, offering unparalleled speed and security. The success of these altcoins is further bolstered by strong community support and network effects. Ethereum, for instance, boasts a robust developer community that is constantly innovating and expanding its capabilities. This collective effort has fortified Ethereum's position as the go-to platform for blockchain-based projects. Similarly, Ripple's network of financial partners and users creates a self-reinforcing ecosystem that enhances its value proposition and market presence.

Strategic partnerships and collaborations have played a significant role in elevating altcoins to greater heights. Cardano, for instance, has forged partnerships with academic institutions to advance blockchain research and education. This collaboration has strengthened Cardano's technological foundation and enhanced its credibility and adoption in academic circles. Chainlink, another prominent altcoin, has collaborated with major tech companies to integrate its decentralized oracle technology, which connects intelligent contracts with real-world data. By facilitating secure and reliable data exchange, Chainlink has become an indispensable component of many blockchain projects, underscoring the importance of strategic alliances in driving innovation and market penetration.

The success of altcoins like Ethereum and Ripple has profoundly impacted the broader cryptocurrency market. Their achievements have sparked increased interest in decentralized applications, encouraging more developers to explore the potential of blockchain technology. This surge in innovation has expanded the scope of what cryptocurrencies can accomplish, attracting a diverse array of projects and investments. The success of these altcoins has also prompted investors to diversify their portfolios beyond Bitcoin, recognizing the potential for growth in alternative cryptocurrencies. As a result, the crypto market has become more dynamic and competitive, with altcoins playing a crucial role in shaping its future. This diversification reflects a growing understanding that the value of cryptocurrencies extends beyond mere speculation, encompassing real-world applications and technological advancements that promise to transform various industries.

7.3 From Rags to Riches: Personal Journeys in Cryptocurrency

In cryptocurrency, the experiences of innovation and change have become inspirational. Take, for example, the tale of a college student who, with little more than curiosity and a modest budget, turned a small investment into a fortune. This student, initially driven by a desire to explore the technological underpinnings of blockchain, began investing in Bitcoin and other cryptocurrencies during their early days. Through careful research, patience, and luck, this individual watched their portfolio swell, eventually reaching millionaire status. This journey underscores cryptocurrency's potential for financial independence, especially when approached enthusiastically and cautiously.

Another remarkable story is that of a single parent who, facing financial struggles, found solace and stability through cryptocurrency investments. Initially skeptical of the digital currency world, this parent began with small, calculated investments, focusing on understanding the market dynamics and trends. Over time, these investments grew, providing a much-needed financial cushion. The newfound wealth enabled them to provide for their family more comfortably, offering a level of security that seemed out of reach before. This narrative highlights that success in cryptocurrency is not limited to a specific demographic; instead, it is available to anyone willing to be educated and take calculated risks.

The backgrounds of successful crypto investors are as diverse as the currencies themselves. From tech enthusiasts already immersed in digital worlds to complete novices who stumbled upon the potential of blockchain, each individual's path to success is unique. Many began their journey with limited resources, driven by the allure of a decentralized financial system that promised opportunity beyond the confines of traditional economic structures. This diversity in starting points emphasizes the accessibility of cryptocurrency as an investment vehicle. It demonstrates that financial hardship is not an insurmountable barrier to entry but rather a challenge that can be overcome with determination and strategic thinking.

Success in the crypto world often hinges on a specific mindset. Risk-taking is common among those who have found wealth through digital currencies. However, it's not about reckless gambling but balancing risk with calculated decision-making. Successful investors carefully analyze market trends, study whitepapers, and remain abreast of technological advancements. They understand that the crypto market's volatility can be both a friend and a foe, and they adapt their strategies accordingly. Continuous learning and adaptation are crucial— they embrace change as a constant, staying flexible in response to shifting market conditions. This mindset allows them to navigate the unpredictable nature of cryptocurrency with confidence and resilience.

These personal success stories have a ripple effect, inspiring others to explore cryptocurrency as a viable path to financial growth. The rise of crypto influencers and educators has contributed significantly to this trend. Individuals who have achieved success often share their experiences and insights, helping to demystify the complexities of digital currencies for newcomers. Knowledgesharing has fostered community and empowerment, encouraging more people to engage with financial literacy and explore new economic possibilities. As more individuals achieve financial independence through crypto, the narrative evolves, drawing on a broader audience eager to learn and participate in this digital revolution.

7.4 Corporate Ventures: How Businesses Are Embracing Crypto

In recent years, corporations have increasingly embraced cryptocurrency, recognizing its potential to revolutionize business operations and enhance profitability. Tesla's strategic decision to invest in Bitcoin and accept it as a form of payment marked a significant shift in the corporate world. By integrating Bitcoin into its financial practices, Tesla made headlines and demonstrated confidence in digital currency as a viable asset. This move allowed Tesla to diversify its treasury holdings while catering to a growing segment of consumers eager to transact in crypto. However, the volatility of Bitcoin prices posed challenges, leading Tesla to halt Bitcoin payments amid environmental concerns related to mining temporarily. This episode underscores the complexities businesses face when navigating the crypto landscape, balancing innovation with the unpredictable nature of digital assets.

Square provides another illustrative case of corporate crypto adoption. The financial services company integrated Bitcoin into its Cash App, allowing users to trade cryptocurrency seamlessly. This integration was driven by a desire to democratize access to digital currency, aligning with Square's mission to empower consumers through financial technology. By facilitating Bitcoin transactions, Square tapped into a burgeoning market, enhancing its service offerings and attracting tech-savvy users. The decision also aligned with Square's investment strategy, as the company allocated some of its assets to Bitcoin, signaling long-term confidence in its value.

For businesses, incorporating cryptocurrency offers numerous advantages, including enhanced payment efficiency and cost savings. By adopting digital currencies, companies can streamline transactions and reduce reliance on traditional banking systems. Crypto payments occur almost instantaneously, providing liquidity and flexibility in financial operations. Yet, the path to integrating cryptocurrency has obstacles. Navigating regulatory compliance remains a significant challenge, as businesses must ensure that their crypto activities adhere to varied and evolving legal frameworks. Moreover, the inherent volatility of cryptocurrencies can impact financial stability, requiring companies to develop robust risk management strategies.

The motivations behind corporate crypto adoption are multifaceted. Companies view digital currencies as a means to innovate within the financial technology sector and gain a competitive edge. Businesses accepting cryptocurrency transactions can place their companies as forwardthinking and adaptable, appealing to a younger, tech-savvy demographic that values digital innovation. The growing consumer demand for crypto payment options cannot be ignored. As more individuals hold and transact in digital currencies, businesses accommodating these preferences can capture a wider market share, enhancing customer satisfaction and loyalty.

Looking to the future, the corporate adoption of cryptocurrency is poised to expand, with several trends on the horizon. One area of growing interest is using blockchain technology for supply chain management. By leveraging blockchain's transparency and security, companies can improve traceability and efficiency in their supply chains, reducing costs and enhancing accountability. Furthermore, the fintech sector is ripe for the expansion of crypto services. As financial institutions seek to innovate and meet the changing needs of consumers, incorporating cryptocurrency solutions is becoming increasingly attractive. The possibilities are vast, from offering crypto-based financial products to integrating blockchain for secure transactions.

As we conclude this chapter, it's clear that corporate ventures into cryptocurrency are reshaping the business landscape, driving innovation, and challenging traditional financial practices. These developments reflect a shift in how businesses operate and underscore the transformative potential of digital currencies in the broader economy. The interplay between corporate adoption and technological advancement will continue evolving and expanding in cryptocurrency as we move forward.

Chapter 8: Engaging with the Cryptocurrency Community

In the vast and dynamic world of cryptocurrency, the sense of community is both a guiding light and a powerful tool. Picture yourself in a thriving marketplace filled with voices discussing the latest trends, sharing insights, and debating the future of digital currencies. This vibrant exchange of ideas is mirrored in the online forums dedicated to cryptocurrency, where enthusiasts from all walks of life gather to connect. One of the most iconic examples is Bitcointalk, a forum that has been pivotal in shaping the crypto landscape. Satoshi Nakamoto founded Bitcointalk as the birthplace of Bitcoin discussions, forging a space where early adopters could collaborate and innovate. It remains a treasure trove of historical insights and ongoing debates, a testament to its enduring influence.

Reddit has also emerged as a vital platform for cryptocurrency conversations, offering a diverse array of subreddits where enthusiasts can explore everything from market analysis to blockchain technology. With communities like r/cryptocurrency and r/Bitcoin, Reddit provides a space for newcomers and seasoned investors to engage in meaningful discussions. These forums are about sharing news, building networks, and learning from the crowd's collective wisdom. Here, you can access real-time updates, discuss market trends, and discover new investment opportunities. The immediacy and breadth of information available make Reddit an important community source for anybody wanting to deepen their understanding of the crypto world.

Participating in these forums offers numerous benefits beyond just information gathering. Engaging with others allows you to ask questions and receive feedback from those who have navigated similar paths. It's like having a mentor available at your fingertips, ready to offer advice and share their experiences. This collaborative environment fosters involvement with others who educate with knowledge about technical insights and investment strategies or a place to discuss the latest crypto news for growth and learning.

To make the most of your forum interactions, it's essential to approach them constructively. Begin by crafting thoughtful questions and comments. Clear and concise inquiries enhance your understanding and encourage meaningful responses. Engaging in discussions with respect and openness can build your credibility within the community, leading to richer interactions and stronger connections. Please share your knowledge and experiences, contribute to conversations, and support others in their inquiries. This reciprocal dynamic enriches the forum experience, allowing you to learn and teach equally.

When seeking forums to join, choose those known for their quality content and active user base. Subreddits like r/cryptocurrency and r/Bitcoin are excellent starting points, offering lively discussions and a wealth of information. Beyond Reddit, platforms like CryptoCompare and TradingView discussions provide specialized forums where market analysis and trading strategies are the focus. These communities are often frequented by experienced traders and analysts, offering insights that can refine your approach to investing. By engaging with reputable forums, you ensure access to reliable information and a community dedicated to advancing the field of cryptocurrency.

Resource List: Reputable Cryptocurrency Forums
- **Bitcointalk**: The original forum for Bitcoin discussions, rich with historical context and ongoing debates.

- **Reddit » r/cryptocurrency**: A leading community for news, discussions, and market trends.

- **Reddit » r/Bitcoin**: Focused on Bitcoin-specific topics, from technical analysis to adoption news.

- **CryptoCompare**: Offers market analysis and trading insights from experienced community members.

- **TradingView Discussions**: A platform for detailed chart analysis and trading strategies.

Engaging with these forums can transform your understanding of cryptocurrency, providing a wealth of knowledge and a network of peers to support your journey.

8.2 Participating in Meetups: Building Your Crypto Network

Picture a room filled with buzzing conversations, the air charged with enthusiasm as people from all corners of the crypto sphere gather to share their passion for digital currencies. Cryptocurrency meetups offer this unique setting, creating opportunities for face-to-face interaction and learning within the community. Unlike the digital interactions of online forums, meetups provide a tangible connection, where ideas can flow freely and relationships can be built in real time. These gatherings can take on various formats, such as workshops, panel discussions, and networking events, each offering its flavor of engagement. Workshops might delve into the technical intricacies of blockchain, while panel discussions could feature industry leaders debating future trends. On the other hand, networking events are perfect for mingling with fellow enthusiasts, exchanging insights, and forging new connections. Whether local or global, meetups are invaluable for anyone looking to deepen their involvement in the crypto world.

Attending crypto meetups can be a game-changer for the knowledge you learn and apply. Imagine shaking hands with industry professionals, conversing with seasoned enthusiasts, and learning directly from expert speakers and panelists. These interactions provide firsthand insights you cannot get from reading articles or watching videos online. Engaging with experts who have navigated the complexities of the crypto space can offer perspectives that challenge your thinking and expand your understanding. Moreover, your connections at these events can open doors to collaborations, mentorships, and even investment opportunities. The crypto community thrives on collaboration; meetups are fertile ground for cultivating these relationships.

To make the most of your meetup experience, preparation is critical. Before attending, take the time to research the event's agenda and speakers and think about the topics you want to explore further. Being prepared ahead of time will help you engage more effectively, ensuring that you make the most of the opportunity to interact with knowledgeable individuals. During the event, be proactive in introducing yourself and participating in discussions. This enhances your learning experience and helps you create a group of individuals with similar interests. After the event, follow up with the people you met through LinkedIn or other social media platforms to maintain and strengthen these new connections. A simple message expressing appreciation for their insights can go a long way in keeping the conversation going.

Finding suitable meetups to attend is essential for maximizing your experience. Websites like Meetup.com and Eventbrite offer a wealth of listings for cryptocurrency events in various locations, allowing you to find ones that match your interests and schedule. These platforms are userfriendly; you can filter events by location, date, and topic to find those most relevant. Social media groups dedicated to local cryptocurrency events can also be excellent resources for discovering meetups in your area. They provide reviews from past attendees and facilitate discussions that can help you decide which meetups to prioritize. Engaging with these platforms keeps you informed about the latest events and connects you with groups willing to give their experiences and knowledge.

Meetups are about more than just learning and networking; they are about being a network of people engaging in advancing financial and technical future. By actively participating in these events, you can gain insights that enhance your understanding, build a network that supports your growth, and contribute to the collective knowledge that drives the crypto space forward. Whether you're a newcomer eager to learn or an intermediate investor wanting to succeed, meetups offer a dynamic and enriching environment that can significantly impact your journey in cryptocurrency.

8.3 Influencers and Thought Leaders: Who to Follow and Why

In the dynamic world of cryptocurrency, influencers and thought leaders hold sway over market perception and trends. These individuals, often with significant online followings, can shift market sentiments with a single tweet or blog post. Consider Andreas Antonopoulos, a stalwart in crypto education and advocacy. His work demystifies complex topics, making them accessible to a broader audience, thus empowering individuals to make informed decisions. Through books, talks, and videos, Antonopoulos provides a foundation for understanding Bitcoin and blockchain, cementing his role as a trusted voice in the community. On a different note, Elon Musk exemplifies the volatile impact of social media in the crypto space. A tweet from Musk can send prices soaring or plunging, illustrating the profound influence these figures can have. While Musk's tweets often spark debate, the attention they garner underscores the power of influencers in shaping crypto narratives.

Following reputable influencers can be immensely beneficial. These thought leaders offer expert analysis and forecasts, guiding followers through the complexities of the crypto market. Engaging with their content provides an opportunity to see how others succeed. For example, learning from someone like Vitalik Buterin, co-founder of Ethereum, offers an insider's perspective on blockchain innovation and the future of decentralized networks. Buterin's insights extend beyond technical aspects; they delve into blockchain technology's philosophical and ethical considerations, encouraging a holistic understanding of its potential. Similarly, Laura Shin, a respected journalist and host of the "Unchained" podcast, conducts in-depth interviews with industry pioneers, offering listeners a chance to hear firsthand accounts of triumphs and challenges in the crypto sphere. These interactions provide valuable lessons and inspiration for those navigating the volatile waters of digital currencies.

However, discerning which influencers to trust requires careful evaluation. Not all voices are created equal; some may be driven by self-interest or hype rather than genuine expertise. A consistent track record is critical. Look for influencers whose predictions and analyses have been accurate over time, proving their deep understanding of the market. Transparency is another crucial criterion; influencers should disclose their affiliations and potential biases, allowing followers to assess the objectivity of their insights. Those who maintain transparency about their holdings and connections are more likely to provide balanced, reliable information. Avoid those whose content leans heavily on sensationalism or promises of guaranteed returns, as these often signal a lack of credibility.

For those seeking a starting point, several influencers stand out for their expertise and balanced perspectives. Vitalik Buterin remains essential for anyone interested in Ethereum and blockchain's broader implications. His thought leadership extends into scalability and governance, offering a comprehensive view of the space. Laura Shin's work in journalism and her podcast give you various opinions inside the industry, making her an invaluable resource for those looking to expand their understanding. By following these thought leaders, you gain extensive knowledge and experience to increase your cryptocurrency investing approach. It's about finding those voices that resonate with your values and goals, helping you navigate the crypto landscape confidently and clearly.

In a world where information is abundant but only sometimes accurate, aligning yourself with credible influencers can be a guiding light. They offer not just data but context and understanding, helping you make sense of the ever-evolving world of digital currencies. As you explore this space, these thought leaders can provide the knowledge and inspiration you need to make informed decisions, contributing to your growth and success in cryptocurrency.

8.4 Navigating Social Media: Reliable Sources vs. Hype

In the fast-paced realm of cryptocurrency, social media serves as both a beacon of information and a minefield of misinformation. Platforms like Twitter and Telegram have emerged as critical players in disseminating real-time news and facilitating discussions. Twitter, in particular, stands out as a primary source for crypto updates and commentary. Influential figures, analysts, and enthusiasts flock to Twitter to share insights, predictions, and breaking news. The immediacy of tweets makes it an invaluable tool for staying informed. Yet, amid the flurry of hashtags and tweets lies the challenge of distinguishing credible information from mere noise. Telegram groups, too, thrive as spaces for community-driven discussions, where enthusiasts gather to exchange ideas and dissect market trends. These groups often offer a more intimate setting, allowing for in-depth conversations and the sharing of diverse perspectives.

Yet, the vast sea of social media information has its pitfalls. The challenge lies in discerning reliable news from the overwhelming tide of clickbait headlines and sensationalism. Critical thinking becomes your most valuable asset in a world where attention spans are short, and headlines are crafted to catch the eye. Identifying the hallmarks of clickbait—such as exaggerated claims or emotionally charged language—can help you navigate this landscape with a discerning eye. Verifying sources before acting on information is crucial. This means checking the credibility of the person or publication behind the news, cross-referencing with other trusted sources, and questioning the motivation behind the information presented. Doing so safeguards yourself against misinformation and ensures your decisions are based on facts rather than hype.

To leverage social media effectively, curating a list of trusted sources and experts is essential.

Follow individuals who have consistently demonstrated accuracy and integrity in their analysis. Engage actively in discussions to gain diverse perspectives, challenge your assumptions, and broaden your understanding. This interactive approach allows you to tap into the community's collective wisdom, providing a richer context for your decisions. Additionally, harness the power of technology to stay updated. Utilize Twitter lists and alerts to organize your feed around specific topics or experts, ensuring you receive timely information without being overwhelmed. These tools help filter the noise, giving you awareness of your decisions and needs. Dedicated Discord channels also offer a focused environment for discussions, bringing together communities with shared interests in a structured manner.

In the digital age, mastering the use of social media requires a blend of skepticism, engagement, and organization. By carefully selecting your information sources and actively participating in discussions, you create a personalized ecosystem of knowledge that empowers you to navigate the intricate world of cryptocurrency confidently. Each tweet, post, or message becomes a puzzle, contributing to a broader understanding of the market's ebb and flow. As you continue to explore the possibilities of digital currencies, remember that social media is a powerful ally when used wisely, offering a window into cryptocurrency's dynamic and ever-evolving landscape.

With these strategies in mind, you can extract the most valuable insights from social media, ensuring you remain informed and agile in your crypto endeavors. As we close this chapter, consider how these tools and strategies can enhance your engagement with the community. In the next chapter, we'll explore the future of cryptocurrency, delving into emerging trends and the knowledge of financial growth and technological advancement.

Chapter 9: Future of Cryptocurrency

Picture this: a bustling city square where every transaction, from a simple coffee purchase to a complex loan agreement, occurs seamlessly without a single human intermediary. This isn't a scene from a futuristic movie but the promise of decentralized finance, or DeFi. DeFi is a revolutionary force transforming the financial landscape by offering decentralized alternatives to traditional financial services. Unlike conventional banking systems relying heavily on centralized institutions, DeFi operates on blockchain technology, eliminating the need for banks and financial institutions as middlemen. This decentralization makes financial services more accessible, transparent, and efficient, ushering in a new era of economic autonomy.

At the heart of DeFi is the concept of smart contracts. These self-executing contracts have terms written into code, enabling transactions without relying on a third party. Imagine renting an apartment through a smart contract that automatically enforces the lease terms—no landlords or agents needed. DeFi platforms leverage these smart contracts to facilitate trustless transactions, where code and cryptography replace traditional trust-based systems. This innovation allows direct lending, borrowing, and user trading, reducing costs and increasing transaction speeds. Platforms like Ethereum have become foundational for DeFi applications, offering the infrastructure to support various financial services.

Ethereum is a pivotal player in the DeFi ecosystem, providing the backbone for many decentralized applications. Its open-source nature and robust, innovative contract capabilities make it an ideal platform for developers looking to innovate. Popular DeFi platforms like Uniswap and Aave exemplify the potential of Ethereum. Uniswap allows tokens to be swapped on their decentralized exchange directly from their wallets without a central authority, enabling seamless and costeffective trading. On the other hand, Aave allows deposits and asset borrowing from their decentralized lending forum and can earn interest, all without traditional financial intermediaries. These platforms illustrate the shift towards decentralized finance, where users have more control over their economic activities.

While DeFi offers numerous benefits, including increased accessibility and financial inclusion, it has challenges. The transparency of blockchain technology ensures that anyone can access financial services through the Internet. This inclusivity democratizes finance, offering opportunities to those traditionally underserved by conventional systems. However, the reliance on smart contracts introduces vulnerabilities. If a smart contract contains a flaw, it can be exploited by scam artists, leading to significant financial losses. Additionally, the regulatory landscape for DeFi remains to be determined as governments grapple with how to oversee decentralized systems. These challenges necessitate careful consideration and risk management for anyone using DeFi platforms.

Real-world use cases demonstrate the transformative potential of DeFi. Consider decentralized stablecoins like DAI, which maintain their value without central control. These stablecoins provide a reliable store of value in the volatile crypto market, facilitating everyday transactions and crossborder payments. Yield farming represents another innovative strategy within DeFi, allowing users to earn high returns on their cryptocurrency holdings. By providing liquidity to DeFi platforms, users receive rewards through additional tokens, creating new opportunities for passive income. These examples highlight how DeFi can disrupt traditional finance, offering alternatives that are faster, cheaper, and more adaptable to the needs of a global audience. **Reflection Section: Exploring Your DeFi Potential**

- **Consider**: What aspects of traditional finance are most restrictive, and how might DeFi offer a solution?

- **Explore**: Research a DeFi platform like Uniswap or Aave. What unique features do they offer, and how could they benefit your financial goals?

- **Reflect**: How comfortable are you with the risks associated with DeFi, such as smart contract vulnerabilities? What precautions can you take?

As you reflect on these questions, consider how the principles of DeFi align with your financial aspirations and whether this new frontier offers the tools you need to achieve them.

9.2 The Role of AI and Blockchain: A Symbiotic Relationship

In the rapidly evolving world of technology, where change is the only constant, the intersection between artificial intelligence (AI) and blockchain stands out as an auspicious development. These two technologies, each revolutionary in its own right, complement each other to enhance efficiency and security. Imagine AI algorithms optimizing blockchain data processing, enabling faster and more accurate data handling. AI can analyze large datasets stored on blockchain networks, identifying patterns and insights impossible for humans to detect. This synergy allows for real-time decision-making and improved operational efficiencies across various sectors.

Blockchain offers AI something equally valuable: secure and immutable data. In AI systems, data integrity is paramount. Blockchain technology ensures that data for training AI models is tamperproof, providing a reliable foundation for building more accurate and trustworthy AI solutions. This immutability is crucial in sectors where data integrity is non-negotiable, such as finance and healthcare. When AI systems operate on blockchain networks, they benefit from a transparent and verifiable data history, enhancing the credibility of AI-driven decisions. This secure data environment is a game-changer in an age when data and information can be infringed upon if not protected and secured.

Integrating AI and blockchain has already begun to reshape industries with innovative applications. Consider AI-driven smart contracts that automate complex decision-making processes. These contracts can execute predefined actions based on real-time data without human intervention, reducing costs and human mistakes. In unusual circumstances, smart contracts may reorder stock automatically when inventory becomes altered, optimizing logistics and reducing waste. In identity verification, blockchain-based systems use AI for fraud detection, analyzing patterns to flag suspicious activities. This combination enhances security and streamlines verification processes, making them more efficient and less prone to human error.

Despite the clear benefits, integrating AI and blockchain poses challenges. Trust and transparency in AI operations improve significantly with blockchain, but technical and ethical hurdles remain. Large-scale implementation requires overcoming issues related to data privacy and interoperability. Additionally, ensuring AI systems operate ethically and without bias is a significant challenge. As AI becomes more autonomous, the need for transparent decision-making processes grows. Blockchain can provide audit trails that offer insights into AI decisions, but ensuring these systems act ethically requires careful oversight and regulation. Balancing innovation with ethical considerations is crucial as these technologies evolve.

Looking to the future, the potential for AI to improve blockchain scalability is an exciting prospect. AI can optimize resource allocation and enhance the performance of blockchain networks, making them faster and more efficient. Additionally, the development of decentralized AI models leveraging blockchain infrastructure is expanding. These models could operate independently, providing decentralized solutions without relying on central authorities. This could lead to more resilient systems operating in diverse environments without central points of failure. As these technologies evolve, their convergence will likely lead to innovations that reshape industries and redefine how we interact with technology. The possibilities and implications are vast as AI and blockchain revolutionize the digital landscape.

9.3 Predictions for the Next Decade: Where Are We Headed?

Cryptocurrency is poised on the brink of transformative change, with experts predicting a future where digital currencies become integral to our financial systems. One of the most significant trends is the increasing institutional adoption of cryptocurrencies. Major financial institutions are beginning to embrace digital assets, recognizing their potential to diversify portfolios and hedge against traditional market volatility. This shift is not merely speculative; it's a strategic move that signals a growing confidence in the stability and viability of cryptocurrencies. As banks, hedge funds, and asset managers incorporate crypto into their offerings, we can expect a ripple effect that accelerates mainstream acceptance and integration.

Another significant development is the rise of CBDCs. Central banks worldwide are accepting digital currencies to complement or replace physical cash. Unlike decentralized cryptocurrencies, Central Bank Digital Currencies (CBDCs) would be issued and regulated by national governments, bridging traditional finance and the digital world. The introduction of CBDCs could streamline monetary policy implementation and enhance the efficiency of payment systems. However, it also raises questions about privacy and government control over individual financial transactions. As these digital currencies gain traction, they could reshape the economic landscape, influencing everything from consumer behavior to global trade dynamics.

The growth of technology is expected to play a critical role in the evolution of cryptocurrencies. Developing more scalable and energy-efficient blockchains is a priority, as current systems often need help with transaction bottlenecks and high energy consumption. Innovations in blockchain technology aim to address these issues, enabling faster and more sustainable transactions. Integration with the Internet of Things (IoT) is another area of focus, promising seamless interactions between devices and digital currencies. Imagine a world where your car automatically pays for parking or your refrigerator orders groceries, all facilitated by blockchain technology. These advancements can revolutionize our interaction with the digital and physical worlds, creating new efficiencies and possibilities.

Regulatory landscapes around the globe are also evolving, with governments striving to balance innovation with consumer protection. Greater clarity in global regulatory frameworks is anticipated, which could provide the certainty needed for the broader adoption of cryptocurrencies. Clear regulations help eliminate current uncertainties that deter potential investors and businesses. However, this shift requires careful consideration to avoid stifling innovation. Regulators face the challenge of creating policies that protect consumers without hindering technological progress. As these frameworks develop, they will likely influence the pace and nature of crypto adoption, shaping how these digital assets are used and perceived.

The societal and economic implications of widespread cryptocurrency adoption are profound. In underserved regions, digital currencies can offer an alternative to traditional banking services. For many, cryptocurrencies provide a way to participate in the global economy, bypassing the limitations of local financial systems. This democratization of finance could empower individuals and communities, fostering economic growth and development. On the other hand, the rise of cryptocurrencies poses challenges to traditional banking and financial institutions. As more people turn to digital currencies, banks may need to adapt their models to remain relevant. This shift could lead to a reimagining of financial services, focusing on digital solutions catering to the needs of a tech-savvy population.

The next decade promises a dynamic and evolving landscape for cryptocurrencies, driven by technological, regulatory, and societal changes. These shifts offer opportunities and challenges, inviting us to rethink our relationship with money and finance in an increasingly digital world.

9.4 Global Adoption: Bridging the Gap Between Traditional and Digital

Imagine a world where digital currencies flow as freely as water, crossing borders and connecting people everywhere. Today, cryptocurrencies are slowly weaving themselves into the fabric of global finance. Some countries stand at the forefront, embracing this digital wave with open arms. Nations like India, Nigeria, and Vietnam have emerged as leaders in crypto adoption, driven by necessity and innovation. These regions have harnessed digital currencies to bypass traditional banking limitations, offering their populations a new gateway to financial services. Governments in these countries are increasingly supporting digital currency use, recognizing the potential to fuel economic growth and financial inclusion. Initiatives range from regulatory frameworks that foster innovation to public-private partnerships that drive technological advancement.

Multiple factors drive this global shift towards cryptocurrency adoption. Technological evolvement has played an important role, with improvements in blockchain infrastructure and internet connectivity paving the way for broader accessibility. The advancement of mobile technology has further democratized availability, allowing individuals outside areas to participate in the digital economy. Growing awareness and education about digital currencies have also contributed to their popularity. As people become more informed about the benefits of cryptocurrencies, they are more willing to explore and adopt them as viable financial tools. This increased understanding has fostered a sense of empowerment, enabling individuals to take control of their financial futures in ways that were previously unimaginable.

However, the path to widespread adoption has its challenges. Regulatory hurdles and inconsistent policies present significant obstacles, often creating uncertainty for users and businesses. Some countries remain skeptical of cryptocurrencies, imposing strict regulations that limit their use. This lack of uniformity can hinder cross-border transactions and deter potential investors, slowing the adoption momentum. Additionally, technological literacy and access in developing regions continue to pose barriers. While mobile technology has made strides, many individuals still need to gain the skills or resources to navigate the digital landscape confidently. Bridging this gap requires targeted efforts to improve digital literacy and infrastructure, ensuring that no one is left behind in the transition to a digital economy.

Innovative strategies are emerging to bridge the gap between traditional and digital systems. Hybrid models that combine the security and familiarity of conventional banking with the flexibility and efficiency of digital assets are gaining traction. These models offer a way to integrate cryptocurrencies into existing financial structures, providing users with a seamless experience. For example, banks are beginning to offer crypto-related services, such as digital wallets and cryptobacked loans, allowing customers to benefit from both worlds. Cross-border payment solutions are also at the forefront of this integration, streamlining international transactions and reducing costs. By leveraging blockchain technology, these solutions facilitate real-time settlements, eliminating the need for intermediaries and providing a more efficient alternative to traditional methods.

The movement towards global cryptocurrency adoption will be almost inevitable. It will be part of the financial future, just like stocks and bonds were in the late 1700s and early 1800s. As technology evolves, the lines between traditional and digital systems blur, creating new opportunities for individuals and businesses worldwide. In this dynamic landscape, those who adapt and embrace change will find themselves at the forefront of a financial revolution, poised to reap the benefits of a truly global economy.

In the next chapter, we will explore how security and privacy concerns shape the future of cryptocurrency, delving into methods that safeguard digital assets and protect user information.

Chapter 10: Ethical and Responsible Investing

Picture a booming cityscape, each building representing a node in the sprawling network of cryptocurrency. As you navigate this urban jungle, it's crucial to be aware of the environmental impact of the digital currencies that underpin this vibrant ecosystem. Cryptocurrency, particularly those utilizing proof-of-work (PoW) mechanisms like Bitcoin, demands significant energy consumption. This has sparked heated discussions about its carbon footprint and ecological consequences. To put it into perspective, the global Bitcoin mining network consumed an astounding 173.42 terawatt-hours of electricity from 2020 to 2021, surpassing the energy consumption of entire countries (Source 1). This level of consumption has resulted in over 85.89 million metric tons of CO_2 emissions, comparable to burning 84 billion pounds of coal (Source 1). Such figures highlight the urgency of addressing the environmental ramifications of cryptocurrency mining as the energy demand continues to grow, intensifying its impact on our planet.

The environmental footprint of Bitcoin mining is exacerbated by its reliance on fossil fuels, with coal contributing to 45% of its energy mix (Source 1). This has led to a water footprint exceeding 1.65 cubic kilometers, surpassing the domestic water use in rural Sub-Saharan Africa (Source 1). Additionally, the land footprint of Bitcoin mining operations spans over 1,870 square kilometers, a staggering area more extensive than Los Angeles (Source 1). These statistics undermine the necessity for sustainable practices within the cryptocurrency industry. Comparatively, traditional financial systems, while also resource-intensive, do not match the concentrated energy usage seen in PoW cryptocurrencies. This raises the question: how can we reduce the environmental impact of digital currencies, ensuring they contribute positively to our world?

Efforts to mitigate the ecological consequences of cryptocurrency are gaining momentum. One promising avenue is transitioning from PoW to proof-of-stake (PoS) consensus mechanisms. PoS indicatively reduces energy consumption by eliminating the need for energy-intensive mining operations (Source 2). Ethereum's recent shift to PoS exemplifies this progress, demonstrating a substantial decrease in energy usage and setting a precedent for other cryptocurrencies. Additionally, the industry is increasingly adopting renewable energy sources for mining operations. Some mining farms are now powered by solar, wind, or hydroelectric energy, reducing their carbon footprint and aligning with global sustainability goals. These initiatives highlight the potential for cryptocurrencies to evolve into more eco-friendly solutions, balancing technological advancement with environmental stewardship.

Collective efforts within the industry are crucial for achieving meaningful environmental change. Partnerships between cryptocurrency companies and environmental organizations are fostering innovative solutions to address environmental concerns. For instance, initiatives like the Crypto Climate Accord aim to decarbonize the industry by encouraging companies to adopt sustainable practices. Industry standards and certifications for eco-friendly mining practices are also emerging, providing benchmarks for companies committed to reducing their ecological impact. By collaborating on these fronts, the cryptocurrency industry can drive positive change, ensuring that digital currencies contribute to a more sustainable future.

As an investor, you have the power to support sustainability in the crypto space. Consider choosing cryptocurrencies with lower energy requirements, such as those using PoS mechanisms or other energy-efficient technologies. Projects like Algorand, Cardano, and Nano are known for their minimal environmental impact and commitment to sustainability (Source 4). Supporting projects prioritizing green initiatives aligns with ethical investing and encourages the industry to adopt sustainable practices. By prioritizing eco-friendly options, you contribute to reducing the environmental footprint of digital currencies, ensuring they benefit both the present and future generations.

Reflection Section: Evaluating Your Crypto's Environmental Impact

- **Assess Your Investments:** Review the cryptocurrencies in your portfolio. Are they energyintensive PoW coins, or do they utilize more sustainable consensus mechanisms like PoS?

- **Research Eco-Friendly Options:** Consider investing in cryptocurrencies known for their sustainability efforts, such as Algorand, Cardano, or Nano (Source 4).

- **Support Green Initiatives:** Actively seek and support projects and exchanges committed to reducing their carbon footprint. Look for industry certifications or partnerships with environmental organizations.

- **Stay Informed:** Keep updated on the environmental impact of cryptocurrencies and emerging sustainable practices within the industry.

These steps can align your investments with your values, supporting a more sustainable and responsible cryptocurrency landscape.

10.2 Social Responsibility: Giving Back Through Crypto

Social responsibility takes on a new dimension in the rapidly evolving landscape of digital currencies. Cryptocurrencies, often viewed through a lens of profit and innovation, can also serve as powerful tools for social good and community empowerment. Imagine a world where digital currencies bridge gaps in financial systems, offering new methods for charitable giving and enhancing transparency in humanitarian efforts. Crypto philanthropy is rising, presenting an opportunity to revolutionize how philanthropic organizations operate. By leveraging blockchain technology, these organizations can ensure that donations reach their intended recipients swiftly and transparently.

One shining example of crypto philanthropy is The Pineapple Fund, an initiative that exemplifies the potential of cryptocurrencies to make a difference. Created by an anonymous Bitcoin investor, the fund gifted over $55 million to various charitable causes, ranging from health and education to environmental conservation. This initiative highlights how digital currency can transcend traditional borders, enabling significant contributions to global issues. Projects like Alice and Giveth are further pushing the boundaries by using blockchain technology to enhance transparency in charitable giving. These platforms allow donors to track their contributions, ensuring funds are used as intended. By fostering trust and accountability, such initiatives encourage more people to engage in philanthropy, knowing their donations are making a tangible impact.

Beyond charity, cryptocurrencies play a pivotal role in financial inclusion, offering unprecedented access to financial services for underserved populations. Traditional banking systems are inaccessible or unreliable in various parts of the world, leaving millions without the means to save, invest, or borrow. Digital currencies and decentralized finance (DeFi) provide an alternative, empowering individuals to manage their finances independently. In regions with scarce banking infrastructure, cryptocurrencies enable transactions without physical banks. For example, digital currencies have become vital tools for economic stability and growth in countries like Kenya and Venezuela, offering a lifeline to those excluded from conventional financial systems.

Case studies from developing countries showcase the transformative power of crypto adoption. In Kenya, the use of cryptocurrencies has expanded rapidly, driven by the need for secure and efficient payment solutions. Mobile money platforms integrated with digital currencies allow users to send and receive funds quickly, facilitating commerce and improving livelihoods. Similarly, in Venezuela, hyperinflation has eroded trust in the local currency, prompting many to turn to cryptocurrencies as a reliable store of value. These examples highlight how digital currencies can empower communities, fostering economic resilience and growth.

To contribute to social causes using cryptocurrency, it's vital to evaluate the transparency and impact of charitable organizations. Look for platforms that provide clear evidence of how funds are used and the outcomes achieved. This transparency builds trust and ensures your contributions make a meaningful difference. Participating in community-driven funding initiatives is another effective way to support social causes. By joining efforts that prioritize collective action and accountability, you can help create sustainable change. These initiatives allow you to engage with a community focused on positive impact that is aligned with your values and aspirations.

Cryptocurrencies offer a unique avenue for social responsibility, blending technology with philanthropy to address pressing global challenges. When you seek the potential of digital currencies in your financial journey, consider how they can be leveraged for social good. You contribute to a more equitable and inclusive world by supporting initiatives that prioritize transparency and impact.

10.3 Ethical Coins: Supporting Sustainable Projects

In the ever-evolving world of cryptocurrency, ethical coins stand out as a beacon for those who seek to align their investments with their values. These digital currencies are designed to focus on sustainability and social impact, setting them apart from traditional cryptocurrencies that often prioritize financial gain over ethical considerations. Ethical coins typically adhere to environmental, social, and governance (ESG) criteria, ensuring they contribute positively to society and the planet. While most cryptocurrencies aim to disrupt financial systems, ethical coins extend this disruption to broader social and environmental issues. By supporting projects committed to these principles, investors can play a part in driving meaningful change.

SolarCoin exemplifies the potential of ethical cryptocurrencies to support sustainable initiatives. This unique digital currency incentivizes renewable energy production by rewarding solar power generators with SolarCoins. Each coin represents a megawatt-hour of solar electricity produced, encouraging the adoption of clean energy and reducing reliance on fossil fuels. The initiative supports environmental sustainability and promotes the growth of renewable energy sectors worldwide. Similarly, impact tokens like those from Plastic Bank aim to tackle pressing global challenges. Plastic Bank's initiative involves collecting and recycling ocean-bound plastic, turning it into currency for impoverished communities. These tokens are a powerful tool to address environmental issues while providing economic opportunities for those in need.

Evaluating the ethical nature of cryptocurrency projects requires a keen eye for transparency and accountability. Investors should examine the project teams behind these coins, ensuring they have a track record of ethical behavior and a clear commitment to their stated goals. The measurable impact of project objectives on sustainability and society is another crucial factor. Ethical investments should deliver tangible benefits through environmental improvements or social advancements. Transparent reporting and regular updates on progress can offer insights into a project's legitimacy and effectiveness, guiding investors to make informed decisions about where to place their support.

Engaging with ethical cryptocurrency communities enhances your understanding and impact in this space. Consider joining forums or groups focused on sustainable crypto initiatives, where discussions revolve around ethical practices and responsible investing. These communities offer a platform for sharing ideas, teaching, and educating others on the latest developments in ethical cryptocurrencies. Supporting ethical initial coin offerings (ICOs) and community-driven projects allows investors to contribute directly to initiatives aligned with their values. Participating in these ventures, you help shape a future where digital currencies are not only financially rewarding but also socially and environmentally responsible.

Checklist: Evaluating Ethical Cryptocurrency Projects
- **Transparency:** Does the project team regularly update stakeholders with straightforward, honest reports?

- **Accountability:** Are the project's goals and outcomes measurable and verifiable?

- **Impact:** What tangible benefits does the project deliver for the environment or society?

- **Community Engagement:** Are there active forums or groups discussing the project, fostering transparency and collaboration?

- **Ethical Track Record:** Does the project team have a history of moral behavior and successful initiatives?

Ethical coins represent a growing movement within the cryptocurrency landscape, offering a path for investors who wish to support projects prioritizing our planet's and society's well-being. By carefully evaluating these projects and engaging with like-minded communities, you can ensure that your investments provide financial returns and contribute to a more sustainable and equitable world.

10.4 Balancing Profit with Principles: Making Responsible Choices

Investing in cryptocurrency doesn't only mean chasing profits but also aligning your investments with your values. This alignment is crucial, as it reflects your ethical beliefs and guides your financial decisions. Economic objectives and moral standards can shape your portfolio, influencing your returns and your impact on society. When you invest in projects that resonate with your values, you support causes that matter to you and potentially reap long-term benefits. Ethical Investing encourages companies to adopt responsible practices, applying transparency and accountability in cryptocurrency. This approach can lead to financial and socially sustainable growth, providing returns measured in dollars and a positive societal impact.

Balancing profit and ethics in cryptocurrency investing requires critical thinking and the will to find diverse goals. One practical approach is diversifying your portfolio to include ethical investments. This strategy spreads risk and aligns your financial activities with your moral compass. Prioritizing projects with transparent and responsible practices is another key tactic. By supporting initiatives that are open about their operations and committed to ethical standards, you help promote a culture of integrity within the crypto community. These projects often demonstrate a commitment to environmental sustainability, social responsibility, or governance principles, offering more than just financial returns. By choosing financial opportunities that fit your ethical beliefs, you can achieve a balance between profit and principle, contributing to a more equitable and responsible financial landscape.

However, ethical investing in crypto has its challenges. Navigating projects with unclear ethical implications can be tricky, as not all projects are forthcoming about their practices or impact. The rapidly changing crypto environment can lead to uncertainties, making it difficult to determine whether a project aligns with your values. Additionally, managing the trade-offs between profitability and principles requires careful consideration. While some ethical investments may offer lower immediate returns, they can deliver significant long-term benefits by fostering sustainable and responsible practices. Balancing these trade-offs involves a willingness to look beyond short-term gains and prioritize investments that contribute positively to society and the environment.

To make informed ethical decisions, you can use practical tools and resources that provide insights into the ethical impact of your investments. Ethical investment platforms and rating systems can help you evaluate projects based on their adherence to environmental, social, and governance criteria. These platforms often provide detailed analyses of a project's impact, transparency, and accountability, allowing you to make decisions that align with your values. Engaging in continuous learning about ethical trends in cryptocurrency is also essential. Keeping abreast of developments in the ethical investment space can enhance your understanding and enable you to adapt to emerging opportunities. By staying informed and leveraging available resources, you can confidently navigate the complexities of ethical investing, ensuring your investments reflect your principles.

In the realm of cryptocurrency, where rapid innovation meets profound responsibility, the choices you make can shape the future. Aligning your investments with personal values allows you to participate in the crypto space with integrity and purpose. As you balance profit with principles, remember that each decision contributes to a broader narrative that envisions a financial system where ethics and economics coexist harmoniously. The journey of ethical investing is not just about financial success but about leaving a legacy of positive change in a world increasingly defined by digital currencies. As you navigate this evolving landscape, let your values guide you, shaping a future where profit and principles thrive together.

Chapter 11: Tools and Resources for Continued Learning

Imagine stepping into a library where every piece of literature had guides to lost treasures of cryptocurrency, each one a gateway to deeper understanding and insight. This is the world of crypto literature—a treasure trove of knowledge waiting to be explored. Whether you're just beginning your journey or seeking to refine your expertise, building a robust crypto library is essential for anyone eager to grasp the intricacies of digital currencies. The right books and articles can illuminate the path, offering you the tools to navigate the ever-evolving landscape of cryptocurrency with confidence and clarity.

Must-Read Books and Articles: Building Your Crypto Library

To truly appreciate the complexity and potential of cryptocurrencies, it's vital to delve into literature that offers both breadth and depth. "Mastering Bitcoin" by Andreas M. Antonopoulos stands as a cornerstone for those with a tech-savvy edge, diving deep into Bitcoin's network, transactions, and security mechanics. Antonopoulos's work is revered for its clarity in explaining intricate technical concepts, making it an indispensable resource for those aspiring to understand Bitcoin's inner workings. On the other hand, "The Age of Cryptocurrency" by Paul Vigna and Michael J. Casey provides a sweeping overview of the digital currency revolution, tracing the origins and evolution of cryptocurrencies while examining their implications on the global financial landscape. This book is perfect for readers seeking a comprehensive yet accessible narrative contextualizing cryptocurrencies within the broader economic framework.

Foundational articles and papers have also significantly shaped the crypto landscape. For instance, Satoshi Nakamoto's Bitcoin whitepaper is not just a technical document but a revolutionary manifesto that sparked the inception of digital currencies. This seminal work lays out the vision for a decentralized currency system, offering insights into the principles that continue to drive the crypto community. Similarly, Vitalik Buterin's writings on Ethereum and smart contracts have been pivotal, elucidating the potential of blockchain technology beyond mere currency transactions—his insights into decentralized applications and programmable contracts open new vistas for innovation and application across various sectors.

When selecting reading material, it's crucial to assess the credibility of authors and publishers. Look into their backgrounds to ensure they possess the expertise and authority to speak on the subject. In-depth information from trustworthy sources can help you choose quality literature that aligns with your learning goals. Absorbing books and news reports that test your mind will improve your understanding. Diversity from different cultural and economic applications will increase your knowledge and acceptance of cryptocurrency's worldwide growth. Exploring technical and nontechnical narratives ensures a balanced knowledge, catering to crypto's theoretical and practical aspects.

Resource List: Building Your Crypto Library
- **"Mastering Bitcoin" by Andreas M. Antonopoulos**: A technical deep dive into Bitcoin's architecture and security.

- **"The Age of Cryptocurrency" by Paul Vigna and Michael J. Casey**: An engaging narrative on the rise of cryptocurrencies.

- **Satoshi Nakamoto's Bitcoin Whitepaper**: The foundational document that introduced the concept of Bitcoin.

- **Vitalik Buterin's Writings**: Explorations of Ethereum's potential and smart contracts.

By curating a library that spans technical manuals, comprehensive overviews, and foundational writings, you equip yourself with a well-rounded understanding of the crypto world. This knowledge empowers you to engage with cryptocurrencies more effectively, making informed decisions as you explore this dynamic and transformative field.

Online Courses and Webinars: Expanding Your Knowledge

In today's digital age, the availability of online courses and webinars has revolutionized how we learn about cryptocurrency, offering flexible and interactive ways to deepen our understanding. Platforms like Coursera and edX provide university-level courses structured to give you a comprehensive grasp of cryptocurrency and blockchain technology. These courses often include lectures from esteemed professors and industry experts, making them an invaluable resource for those who prefer a more academic approach to learning. Meanwhile, Udemy offers many practical guides and tutorials catering to varying skill levels. Whether you're a beginner looking for an introduction or an experienced trader seeking advanced strategies, Udemy's wide range of topics ensures something for everyone.

The interactive nature of webinars adds another layer to the learning experience. Unlike traditional courses, webinars offer real-time learning opportunities, allowing you to engage directly with experts in the field. This interaction often includes live Q&A

sessions where you can pose questions and receive immediate feedback from seasoned professionals. Such opportunities enhance understanding and provide exclusive insights that might not be available elsewhere. Additionally, webinars often feature discussions on the latest trends and developments in cryptocurrency, keeping you informed and up-to-date with the ever-evolving market dynamics.

When choosing courses and webinars, ensuring they align with your learning objectives and skill level is crucial. Start by carefully evaluating the course outline and learning outcomes. A wellstructured course should offer clear goals and an analytical advancement of topics that build on your existing knowledge. It's also important to check the credentials of the demonstrators. Look for courses taught by industry professionals or academics with a strong background in cryptocurrency. Analysis and testimonials from past participants can offer extra discernment into the effectiveness and quality of the course material. Considering these factors, you can choose educational resources that enhance learning and provide value.

The landscape of online education offers both free and paid options, ensuring access to quality learning regardless of budget constraints. Platforms like Khan Academy offer free introductory courses that cover the basics of cryptocurrency, making them a great starting point for beginners. These courses often break down complex topics into manageable lessons, fostering a solid foundation in digital currencies. For those seeking more in-depth exploration, there are advanced paid courses available that offer certifications upon completion. These courses often dive deeper into specific areas of cryptocurrency, such as blockchain development or financial applications, providing a thorough understanding that can be beneficial for career advancement.

Courses like MIT Media Lab's Cryptocurrency Course, highlighted in Source 2, offer an extensive curriculum led by industry experts like Gary Gensler and Neha Narula. Although these courses may require a financial investment, the depth of knowledge and certification they offer can be invaluable for serious learners. On the other hand, platforms like edX and Coursera provide free options for auditing courses, with the opportunity to upgrade for a fee if certification is desired. This affability lets you adapt your learning experience to suit your needs, balancing cost with the depth of content.

Online courses and webinars represent a dynamic and accessible way to expand cryptocurrency knowledge. They provide the tools and insights needed to navigate the complexities of digital finance effectively. Through interactive learning and expert-led content, these resources empower you to engage confidently with the world of cryptocurrency.

Analytical Tools: Enhancing Your Trading Skills

Navigating the cryptocurrency market without the right tools is like trying to sail without a compass. To make informed decisions, you need analytical tools that provide clarity and insight into market movements. TradingView is a prevalent choice for many traders, offering a robust charting and technical analysis platform. Its comprehensive features include various chart types and technical indicators that help you track price movements and identify potential trading opportunities. With TradingView, you can customize your charts to focus on the data most relevant to your strategy, whether moving averages, Bollinger Bands, or Relative Strength Index (RSI). This flexibility allows you to accommodate your analysis to suit your trading style, whether you're a day trader seeking quick profits or a long-term investor looking for trends.

CoinGecko is another indispensable resource, providing detailed market data and price tracking for thousands of cryptocurrencies. This platform offers real-time data on market capitalization, trading volume, and price changes, allowing you to stay updated on market trends. CoinGecko's user-friendly interface makes it easy to compare cryptocurrencies and assess their performance over time. Using CoinGecko, you can identify emerging trends and make data-driven decisions aligning with your investment goals. Whether you're tracking the price of Bitcoin or exploring new altcoins, CoinGecko provides the information you need to make informed choices.

Beyond basic charting and data analysis, advanced trading platforms offer features that enhance your decision-making capabilities. Customizable chart indicators and alerts allow you to set specific criteria for monitoring market conditions. These features facilitate you to receive notifications when certain thresholds are met, such as a moving average crossover or a sudden price spike. Many platforms offer historical data analysis and backtesting features that let you exercise your trading strategies against past market conditions. By analyzing how your strategy would have performed in different scenarios, you can refine your approach and increase your chances of success in live trading.

Integrating AI and machine learning in trading tools is becoming more prevalent as technology evolves. Algorithmic trading bots use AI-driven algorithms to execute trades based on predefined criteria, allowing you to automate your trading strategy and minimize emotional decision-making. These bots can analyze boundless amounts of data in real-time, identifying patterns and trends that may not be immediately apparent to people. Machine learning models take this further by predicting market trends based on historical evidence and current market conditions. You can optimize your trading strategies by leveraging AI and machine learning and rapidly adapt to changing market dynamics.

Choosing the right tools for your trading necessities requires careful consideration of your goals and experience level. Assess each tool's user interface and ease of use to ensure it aligns with your preferences and trading style. An intuitive and easy-to-navigate tool can save you costly time and reduce the risk of errors. Additionally, evaluate the compatibility of each tool with your existing trading setup. Whether you trade on a desktop or mobile device, ensure that the tools you choose integrate seamlessly with your preferred platform and support your trading activities.

The right combination of analytical tools can increase your trading skills and improve your decision-making practice. You can accomplish a competitive edge in the ever-evolving cryptocurrency market by leveraging platforms like TradingView and CoinGecko, advanced features and AI-driven tools. As you explore these resources, remember that continuous learning and adaptation are the keys to successful trading. Stay informed, stay curious, and let your analytical tools guide you toward achieving your trading goals.

Glossaries and Dictionaries: Navigating Crypto Terminology

Knowledge of cryptocurrency terminology is critical for anyone looking to effectively engage with the digital currency space. The crypto world is laden with jargon that may be as perplexing as trying to decode a foreign language. Terms like "hash rate," "blockchain," and "smart contracts" are foundational yet often misunderstood. Clear comprehension of these terms is vital, not only for participating in discussions but also for interpreting technical documents and contracts. It would help if you grasped the correct terminology to avoid losing yourself in conversations or misinterpreting critical information that could impact your investments. It's not just about knowing the words but their implications and uses in real-world applications.

Comprehensive glossaries and dictionaries are invaluable for mastering this complex language. Investopedia's cryptocurrency glossary is a great starting point for beginners, providing straightforward definitions that break down complicated concepts into digestible pieces. For those who crave a more specialized resource, "CryptoDictionary" offers detailed explanations tailored to the intricate aspects of digital currencies. These resources serve as reliable companions, ensuring you have a trustworthy reference to consult whenever you encounter unfamiliar terms. Routinely consulting these glossaries can build a robust vocabulary that enhances understanding and boosts your confidence in navigating the crypto landscape.

Mastering crypto language requires more than passive reading; it involves active engagement and ongoing practice. One effective method is regularly reviewing terms and concepts, reinforcing memory, and deepening understanding. Flashcards and mnemonic devices can be especially helpful in retaining new vocabulary. Flashcards allow you to analyze your knowledge and track progress, while mnemonic devices offer creative ways to remember complex terms. Writing things down can further solidify your grasp of the material, turning abstract concepts into concrete knowledge. Integrating these techniques into your learning routine can transform a baffling task into a manageable and rewarding endeavor.

Active use is another powerful method to enhance your command of crypto terminology. Engaging in discussions and debates about cryptocurrency topics can solidify your understanding and reveal gaps in your knowledge. By participating in community forums and online meetings, you can apply what you've learned and gain insights from others in the field. Writing blog posts or articles about crypto topics can also reinforce your comprehension, as explaining concepts to others helps clarify your understanding. These activities improve your fluency in crypto language and connect you with a broader community of enthusiasts and experts who share your interests.

In this chapter, we've explored the significance of mastering cryptocurrency terminology, highlighted reliable resources for learning, and explored strategies for effective language acquisition. As you continue to build your knowledge and confidence, remember that understanding the language of crypto is a journey of continuous learning. By embracing these tools and techniques, you equip yourself to navigate the crypto landscape with clarity and purpose, ready to engage with the opportunities and challenges it presents.

As we conclude this chapter, reflecting on the tools and resources discussed, you are better equipped to enhance your crypto knowledge and skills. In the next chapter, we will delve into personal growth and mindset, exploring how to cultivate the right attitude for success in the eve-revolving world of cryptocurrency.

Chapter 12: Personal Growth and Mindset

Imagine a landscape constantly shifting beneath your feet. This is the cryptocurrency market, where change is the only constant, and adaptation is critical. In such an environment, cultivating a growth mindset is not just beneficial; it's essential. Coined by psychologist Carol Dweck, a growth mindset is the belief that adeptness and intelligence can be developed through devotion and hard work. In crypto, this translates to seeing each challenge as an opportunity to become educated, innovate, and grow. Unlike a fixed mindset, which sees failure as a setback, a growth mindset embraces it as a stepping stone to success. This perspective is crucial, as the crypto market's volatility can be daunting. Embracing new technologies and being open to change transforms potential obstacles into pathways for advancement.

To develop this mindset, consider the power of self-reflection. Taking time to assess your experiences and decisions helps build resilience. Mindfulness practices, such as meditation, can also foster a calm and focused mind, enabling you to navigate uncertainties. Engaging with diverse viewpoints broadens your understanding and exposes you to new possibilities. Whether through podcasts, books, or discussions, welcoming different perspectives enriches your knowledge and equips you with the tools to tackle challenges creatively. By adopting these strategies, you cultivate a mindset that thrives on growth and innovation, setting the stage for success in the everevolving crypto landscape.

Constant learning is a cornerstone of personal growth, especially in a field as dynamic as cryptocurrency. Being afloat of the latest market trends and technological advancements is paramount. The crypto world evolves rapidly, with new projects and innovations emerging regularly. Pursuing educational opportunities, such as online courses or certifications, keeps your skills sharp and relevant. These endeavors enhance your expertise and open windows to new opportunities. By committing to lifelong learning, you position yourself as a knowledgeable participant in the crypto space, ardent to adapt and capitalize on emerging trends.

Real-world examples abound of individuals who have harnessed a growth mindset to achieve remarkable success in crypto. Entrepreneurs often pivot their projects based on market feedback, demonstrating adaptability and resilience. This flexibility allows them to refine their offerings and meet evolving demands, ultimately leading to sustained success. Investors, too, adjust their strategies in response to market shifts. They optimize their portfolios and maximize returns by viewing each market fluctuation as a chance to learn and evolve. These examples illustrate the transformative power of a growth mindset, showcasing how embracing change can lead to significant achievements.

Reflection Section: Embracing a Growth Mindset in Crypto

Take a moment to reflect on your experiences in the crypto world. Consider challenging situations you've faced and how they presented growth opportunities. Jot down moments when embracing change led to positive outcomes. Identify areas where a growth mindset could enhance your approach. Use these reflections to guide your journey in the dynamic world of cryptocurrency, embracing each challenge with curiosity and determination.

12.2 Learning from Mistakes: Turning Setbacks into Success

In cryptocurrency investing, mistakes are as inevitable as the market's volatility. These setbacks, however, are not the end of the road. They are part of the learning process. It's natural to feel the sting of a loss, especially when the stakes are high. Yet, each misstep offers a chance to glean insights, refine strategies, and move forward with greater wisdom.

Embracing failures as learning opportunities rather than roadblocks can transform how you approach investing. This perspective allows you to see losses not as failures but as valuable lessons that contribute to your growth as an investor. In a market where change is constant, normalizing loss experience is crucial.
Understanding that everyone experiences setbacks can help you maintain perspective and build resilience.

Structured approaches can be invaluable for effectively learning from mistakes. Conducting postmortem analyses of failed trades is one such method. This involves examining each aspect of a trade to understand what went wrong and why. By identifying patterns and behaviors that led to mistakes, you can develop strategies to avert repeating them. It would help if you had made a better decision influenced by market hype or overlooked critical information. Perceiving these patterns enables you to make informed decisions in the future. This analytical approach transforms each setback into a step forward, allowing you to refine your investment strategy continuously. Over time, this reflection and adjustment process can significantly Improve your decision-making and overall success in the crypto market.

Resilience and perseverance are vital to transforming setbacks into stepping stones for success. Building mental toughness through difficulty is essential. It's about developing the ability to keep going even when things don't go as planned. This resilience is about enduring losses and using them as a foundation to build. Developing new strategies based on past experiences can lead to innovative approaches that set you apart from other investors. Each setback offers a unique opportunity to reassess your approach and adapt to the changing market landscape. This adaptability is crucial in a field as dynamic as cryptocurrency, where the ability to pivot and adjust can be the distinction between success and stagnation. Embracing resilience allows you to maneuver the market's volatility confidently and poise.

The cryptocurrency world is filled with stories of individuals who have overcome setbacks to achieve remarkable success. Many investors have rebounded after significant losses, using their experiences to make better decisions and achieve their financial goals. These stories are powerful reminders that failure is often a precursor to success. Entrepreneurs in the crypto space have also faced their share of challenges, pivoting their ventures based on feedback and market changes.
Their ability to adapt and persevere has led to innovative projects and successful businesses.

These examples illustrate the transformative power of resilience and the importance of learning from mistakes. They demonstrate that setbacks while challenging, can be harnessed as valuable tools for growth and progress in the ever-evolving world of cryptocurrency.

Case Study: Resilience in the Face of Loss

Consider an investor who faced a significant loss during a market downturn. Instead of retreating, they analyzed their mistakes, identified emotional decision-making patterns, and adjusted their strategy. Focusing on long-term investments and diversifying their portfolio, they rebounded, turning initial setbacks into substantial gains. This story exemplifies how resilience and thoughtful reflection can pave the way for success in the cryptocurrency market.

12.3 Staying Motivated: Setting Goals and Achieving Them

In cryptocurrency, setting clear and achievable goals serves as your compass. It guides your decisions and actions, motivating you amidst the market's ebbs and flows. Establishing goals provides direction, helping you focus on what truly matters on your path. The SMART criteria— Specific, Measurable, Achievable, Relevant, and Time-bound—offer a framework for crafting realistic and inspiring goals. These elements ensure that your goals are not vague but concrete targets you can actively pursue. Aligning these goals with your personal values and financial aspirations adds another layer of motivation. When your goals resonate with your core beliefs and long-term dreams, they become more than a checklist; they transform into a driving force that propels you forward, even when the market gets turbulent.

Maintaining encouragement requires more than just setting goals; it involves cultivating a mindset that keeps you engaged and focused. Visualization exercises can be powerful mechanisms in this process. By vividly imagining your success, you create a mental image of what you're striving for, making it feel attainable and tangible. This technique can enhance your motivation, especially during challenging times. Additionally, forming accountability partnerships with peers or mentors provides external motivation and support. Having someone to share your progress with, discuss challenges, and celebrate victories can reinforce your commitment to your goals. These relationships provide encouragement and perspective, helping you stay on track when distractions or doubts arise.

Together, these strategies create a robust support system that nurtures your motivation and resilience.

Tracking progress is another crucial aspect of goal achievement. Using apps and tools designed for goal tracking can simplify this process, offering a clear overview of your accomplishments and areas needing attention. Periodically reviewing your goals allows you to assess your progress and make necessary adjustments. This flexibility ensures that your goals remain relevant and aligned with your current situation, adapting to changes in the market or your circumstances. By continuously evaluating your progress, you stay engaged with your goals, making informed decisions that support your long-term aspirations. This dynamic approach to goal setting and tracking fosters a proactive mindset, empowering you to navigate challenges confidently and clearly.

Stories of individuals who have successfully set and achieved significant goals in the crypto space offer valuable insights and inspiration. Consider traders who have reached financial independence through disciplined goal-setting. By establishing clear financial targets and adhering to a strategic plan, they navigated the market's volatility and achieved their aspirations. Their discipline and focus testify to the power of effective goal-setting. Similarly, developers who launched successful blockchain projects demonstrate the importance of aligning goals with passion and innovation. Their ability to envision a project set specific milestones, and work diligently towards it highlights the transformative potential of clear and purposeful goals. These examples illustrate how setting and achieving goals can lead to remarkable accomplishments, inspiring you to pursue your objectives with determination and enthusiasm.

12.4 The Journey Ahead: Your Path to Financial Independence

Imagine a future where financial independence is not a fantasy but a reality. Cryptocurrency offers a unique path to achieve this by allowing strategic engagement in the market. Over time, building a diversified portfolio is critical. This involves spreading investments across various cryptocurrencies to mitigate risks and capitalize on growth opportunities. A well-rounded portfolio acts like a safety net, cushioning against market volatility while enhancing potential returns. Diversification isn't merely about picking a random assortment of assets; it requires careful analysis and understanding of each crypto's potential and role in your financial strategy. In doing so, you create a robust foundation that supports long-term growth and stability.

In addition to a diversified portfolio, exploring passive income opportunities can accelerate your journey to financial freedom. Decentralized Finance (DeFi) platforms offer avenues for earning through lending, yield farming, and liquidity provision. Staking, another powerful strategy, involves holding cryptocurrencies in a wallet to support network operations, earning rewards in return. These methods allow your assets to work for you, generating income without constant market monitoring. As you delve into these opportunities, you must remain informed about the risks and rewards associated with each. Passive income isn't passive in the sense of being effortless; it requires ongoing diligence and strategic planning to ensure sustainable growth.

Achieving financial independence through cryptocurrency demands a disciplined mindset. Discipline is your ally, guiding you through the market's highs and lows. Patience, too, plays a vital role, as rushing into decisions often leads to mistakes. Informed decision-making is the foundation of successful investing. Access to data, insights, and the willingness to adapt your strategy as needed are essential components of this process. Long-term thinking and planning are vital, allowing you to see beyond immediate fluctuations and focus on overarching financial goals. Balancing risk with strategic investments is a delicate dance, requiring constant evaluation and adjustment to maintain the desired trajectory.

Once financial independence is within grasp, the challenge shifts to maintaining it. Regularly reassessing your investment strategies and asset allocations is crucial. Markets evolve, and what applied yesterday may not apply tomorrow. You can adapt to innovations and seize new opportunities by staying engaged and informed. Continuing education remains a priority, ensuring you stay ahead of trends and technological advancements. Whether through courses, webinars, or community engagement, learning is a lifelong endeavor that keeps you sharp and adaptable. This ongoing commitment to growth and adaptation fortifies your financial stability, helping you sustain independence for the long haul.

The stories of individuals who have accomplished financial independence through cryptocurrency are potent inspirations. Early adopters who recognized Bitcoin's potential early on have seen their investments grow exponentially. Their foresight and willingness to embrace new technology paved the way for financial freedom. Innovators who built successful crypto-related businesses also demonstrate the vast potential within this space. By determining gaps in the market and offering solutions, they've created sustainable ventures that contribute not only to their wealth but also to the broader crypto ecosystem. These stories highlight the diverse paths to financial independence, each marked by vision, determination, and a keen understanding of the crypto landscape.

As we conclude this chapter, consider how these insights can guide your journey toward financial independence through cryptocurrency. You confidently navigate the dynamic crypto market by embracing strategic engagement, disciplined planning, and continuous learning. With each decision, you move closer to a future where financial freedom is not just an aspiration but a reality.

Conclusion

As we reach the end of this journey, it's vital to reflect on the wealth of knowledge we've explored together. We began by unraveling the complexities of the cryptocurrency landscape, demystifying the core concepts that underpin digital currencies. We've laid a solid foundation from understanding blockchain technology to recognizing various cryptocurrencies beyond Bitcoin. Our exploration then ventured into strategies for investing wisely and securely, highlighting the importance of choosing reputable exchanges and understanding the role of wallets in safeguarding your digital assets. As we ventured further, we delved into the intricacies of technical analysis, offering insights into reading charts and identifying market cycles. Finally, we explored future trends, ethical investing, and cryptocurrency's evolving role in the global financial ecosystem. This comprehensive journey was designed to give you the knowledge and confidence to pilot the cryptocurrency world effectively.

Throughout this book, key takeaways have been emphasized to ensure you leave with actionable insights. The importance of securing your cryptocurrency investments cannot be understated. You can protect your digital assets from risks by performing robust security measures, such as twofactor authentication and cold storage solutions.

Informed decision-making is another critical lesson, underscoring the need to blend technical and fundamental analysis to make sound investment choices. Ethical considerations have also been highlighted, encouraging you to invest in projects that align with your financial goals and personal values. You can confidently engage with the cryptocurrency market by remembering these lessons.

This book was born from a vision to empower you to invest in cryptocurrency safely and wisely. My years of experience trading on platforms like Robinhood and Coinbase have shown me the value of practical advice grounded in real-world experience. Whether you're a newcomer to the crypto world or a seasoned investor, the goal was to provide clarity and new perspectives. By analyzing complex topics into digestible insights, I hope to have made this fascinating world more accessible to you.

Consistent education is crucial in the ever-evolving landscape of cryptocurrency. The market is dynamic, and being informed is essential to success. Please continue your education, leveraging the resources and tools provided in this book. Whether through online courses, webinars, or engaging with the crypto community, continuous learning will keep you at the forefront of industry developments. Adaptability and a willingness to embrace new knowledge are your allies in this journey.

The inspiring real-life success stories shared throughout these pages serve as motivation. From early adopters turning modest investments into fortunes to individuals achieving financial independence, these stories illustrate the vast potential within the cryptocurrency space. No matter where you start, the opportunities for growth and success are boundless. Let these stories inspire you to take bold steps and pursue your path in the crypto world.

Now, I urge you to take action. Apply the strategies and insights gained from this book to your investment journey. Whether setting up a secure account, exploring new investment opportunities, or engaging with the community, you are ready. You have the knowledge and confidence to navigate the complexities of cryptocurrency.

Thank you for embarking on this journey with me. I invite you to join the broader cryptocurrency community. Attend meetups, participate in forums, and share your experiences. You can continue to learn and contribute to the vibrant crypto landscape by engaging with others.

Looking forward, the future of cryptocurrency is bright and filled with possibilities. Envision your role in shaping this dynamic space. With your newfound knowledge, you can contribute positively to the growth and innovation of digital finance. Embrace the opportunities ahead and continue to explore cryptocurrency's boundless potential.

Important Note From The Author

I want to share some of my cryptocurrency investing experiences and knowledge with my readers. At the start of my first ventures in cryptocurrency, I could have made 200000 dollars in 2 days from a $4000 investment I made on a start-up crypto coin, but I did not because I got greedy and thought it would keep going up. I also got scammed and lost $4000 on another coin that promised high returns, but it turned out that I gave them my secret recovery phrase to recover my losses, only to find out that they were stealing my coins from my MetaMask wallet. I was watching them deplete my account live. I immediately caught on and saved half of my losses by immediately transferring the other coins to my Trust Wallet. You should also have at least two wallets for transferring crypto to and fro when necessary. MetaMask, Trust Wallet, and Coinbase are good wallets to own. (These wallets generate a secret recovery phrase comprising a list of 12- 24 words; make sure you never lose them because you will lose all your cryptocurrency in those wallets; it is crucial). Therefore, I have learned from my aspirations and mistakes to be conservative, savvy, and patient. This is why I wrote this book: so that you may be aware of and educated about cryptocurrency.

My advice is based only on my education and experience. Do your due diligence and seek more advice from legal professionals. I recommend only investing in secure coins, usually up to the top-ranked 200 cryptocurrencies like Bitcoin, Ethereum, Binance, XRP, Cronos, IOTX, etc. If you want to make money safely and securely, the long term is the best time to use the dollar cost averaging method. Crypto prices have medium to high volatility market cycles depending on news events and social media persuasion. I only recommend you buy at the bottom when the market drops and when you sell only when it peaks. Remember, only use money you will not miss and will not feel hardship when the market goes down. Depending on your budget, only invest excess money you will not notice. I recommend practicing with small amounts of money until you become comfortable. You can open an account at cryptocurrency exchanges like Robinhood, Crypto.com, and Coinbase for as little as 100 dollars. Use this amount to deposit and practice trading-- buying and selling cryptocurrency. After selling your coins, practice withdrawing your funds in and out of your account. Finally, once you feel comfortable and experienced, you are now ready to start investing and saving for your future in the Cryptocurrency World.

References

- *Blockchain Facts: What Is It, How It Works, and How It Can ...*
  https://www.investopedia.com/terms/b/blockchain.asp

- *Bitcoin, altcoins, meme coin differences explained - CNBC*
  https://www.cnbc.com/2024/05/29/bitcoin-altcoins-meme-coin-differencesexplained.html#:~:text=Altcoins%2C%20also%20known%20as%20alternative,a%20specif ic%20purpose%20in%20mind.

- *Proof of Work VS Proof of Stake in Blockchain*
  https://glair.ai/post/proof-of-work-vs-proofof-stake-in-blockchain

- *The Pillars of Blockchain Security: Decentralization and ...*
  https://blockapps.net/blog/thepillars-of-blockchain-security-decentralization-and-encryption/

- *Best Crypto Exchanges and Apps for October 2024*
  https://www.investopedia.com/bestcrypto-exchanges-5071855

- *Hot Wallet vs. Cold Wallet: What's the Difference?*

https://www.investopedia.com/hotwallet-vs-cold-wallet-7098461

- *How to Open a Crypto Account | Banks.com* https://www.banks.com/articles/investing/cryptocurrency/open-account/

- *Embracing Two-Factor Authentication for Enhanced ...* https://www.tripwire.com/state-ofsecurity/embracing-two-factor-authentication-enhanced-account-protection

- *Complete Beginner's Guide to Reading Crypto Charts* https://coinbureau.com/education/how-to-read-a-crypto-chart/

- *Bull vs. Bear Markets: What's The Difference?* https://www.investopedia.com/insights/digging-deeper-bull-and-bear-markets/

- *CoinGecko is one of the best crypto analysis tools offering comprehensive digital currency data. You can use it to gain a deeper ...* https://ninjapromo.io/best-crypto-tools-foranalysis-trading-research

- *How to Deal With Fear of Missing Out (FOMO) in Crypto Trading* https://blog.ueex.com/fomo-in-crypto-trading/

- *Long-Term vs Short-Term Crypto Investment Strategies* https://medium.com/@TDXbiz/long-term-vs-short-term-crypto-investment-strategies2f8e95143ed5

- *Ultimate Guide to Diversifying Your Crypto Portfolio* https://www.honeybricks.com/learn/crypto-portfolio-diversification

- *How To Analyze Altcoins Before Investing In Them* https://prestmit.io/blog/how-to-analyzealtcoins-before-investing-in-them

- *The Risks and Rewards of ICO Investing* https://www.bitget.com/academy/the-risks-andrewards-of-ico-investing

-

- *Understanding Private Keys: Crypto Safety* https://komodoplatform.com/en/academy/bitcoin-private-key/

- *Common cryptocurrency scams and how to avoid them* https://www.kaspersky.com/resource-center/definitions/cryptocurrency-scams

- *A guide to wallet security & best practices:* https://algorand.co/learn/wallet-security-bestpractices

- *Privacy Coins Explained - A Complete Guide for Beginners* https://www.tokenmetrics.com/blog/privacy-coins

- *Digital assets | Internal Revenue Service* https://www.irs.gov/businesses/smallbusinesses-self-employed/digital-assets

- *Best Crypto Tax Software Of October 2024* https://www.forbes.com/advisor/taxes/bestcrypto-tax-software/

- *SEC Continues to Regulate Cryptocurrency Through ...* https://www.troutman.com/insights/seccontinues-to-regulate-cryptocurrency-throughrecord-high-enforcement-efforts.html

-

- *What Are the Legal Risks to Cryptocurrency Investors?* https://www.investopedia.com/tech/what-are-legal-risks-cryptocurrency-investors/

- *Bitcoin Pizza Day: Celebrating the 10000 BTC Pizza Order* https://www.investopedia.com/news/bitcoin-pizza-day-celebrating-20-million-pizza-order/

- *Smart Contracts Market Size, Share, Value, Global Report ...* https://www.fortunebusinessinsights.com/smart-contracts-market-108635 *Ripple: Driving Global Payments with Blockchain* https://fintechmagazine.com/articles/ripple-driving-global-payments-with-blockchain

- *The impact of Tesla's Bitcoin investment and its plans to ...* https://sciendo.com/pdf/10.2478/picbe-2021-0007

- *Top 35 Cryptocurrency Forums in 2024* https://forums.feedspot.com/cryptocurrency_forums/

- *30 Best Crypto Conferences & Events to Attend in 2024* https://ninjapromo.io/best-cryptoconferences

-

- *Cointelegraph Top 100 | 2023* https://cointelegraph.com/top-people-in-crypto-andblockchain-2023

- *Crypto Social Media Scams: How to Stay Safe* https://www.certik.com/resources/blog/crypto-social-media-scams-how-to-stay-safe

- *The Impact of Decentralized Finance on Traditional Banking* https://www.openware.com/news/articles/the-impact-of-decentralized-finance-ontraditional-banking

- *Blockchain and AI - Use Cases* https://blog.chain.link/blockchain-ai-use-cases/

- *Mid-Year Review: VanEck's 15 Crypto Predictions for 2024* https://www.vaneck.com/us/en/blogs/digital-assets/matthew-sigel-mid-year-reviewvanecks-15-crypto-predictions-for-2024/

- *The 2023 Global Crypto Adoption Index* https://www.chainalysis.com/blog/2023-globalcrypto-adoption-index/

- *The Environmental Footprint of Bitcoin Mining Across the   ...*

- https://agupubs.onlinelibrary.wiley.com/doi/full/10.1029/2023EF003871

- *Proof of stake vs. proof of work: What you need to know* https://www.fidelity.com/learningcenter/trading-investing/proof-of-work-vs-proof-of-stake

- *The Giving Block's 2023 Annual Report Reveals Crypto ...* https://www.nonprofitpro.com/article/the-giving-blocks-2023-annual-report-revealscrypto-philanthropy-on-the-rise/.

- *15 Environmentally Sustainable Cryptocurrencies To Invest ...* https://esgnews.com/15environmentally-sustainable-cryptocurrencies-to-invest-in-right-now/

- *Best Cryptocurrency Books: From Fundamentals to Trading* https://bitsgap.com/blog/bestcryptocurrency-books-from-fundamentals-to-trading

- *8 Best Cryptocurrency Courses Online in 2024* https://hackr.io/blog/best-cryptocurrencycourses

36 Best Crypto Tools for Analysis, Trading & Research in ...

- https://ninjapromo.io/bestcrypto-tools-for-analysis-trading-research

- *Crypto Glossary of Terms And Jargon* https://coinmarketcap.com/academy/glossary

- *7 Ways to Develop A Growth Mindset for Long-Term   ...* https://passiveincomemd.com/7ways-to-develop-a-growth-mindset-for-long-term-investing-success/

- *Cryptocurrency Market Size, Share & Growth Report,   2030* https://www.grandviewresearch.com/industry-analysis/cryptocurrency-market-report

- *Bitcoin's Resilience: Thriving Amidst Global Uncertainty* https://medium.com/roymavila/bitcoins-resilience-thriving-amidst-global-uncertainty0f860940ca52

- *Crypto Millionaires: Stories of Early Adopters* https://vezgo.com/blog/crypto-millionaires/